my **revis**

EDEXCEL AS
UK GOVERNMENT & POLITICS

Neil McNaughton

Series Editor: Eric Magee

HODDER
EDUCATION

With thanks to all the students whose valuable feedback helped develop this book.

Hodder Education, an Hachette UK company, 338 Euston Road, London NW1 3BH

Orders

Bookpoint Ltd, 130 Milton Park, Abingdon, Oxfordshire OX14 4SB
tel: 01235 827827
fax: 01235 400401
e-mail: education@bookpoint.co.uk
Lines are open 9.00 a.m.–5.00 p.m., Monday to Saturday, with a 24-hour message answering service. You can also order through the Hodder Education website: www.hoddereducation.co.uk

© Neil McNaughton 2012
ISBN 978-1-4441-5487-0

First printed 2012
Impression number 5
Year 2017 2016 2015 2014

Cover photo reproduced by permission of ferkelraggae/Fotolia

Typeset by Datapage, India
Printed in Spain

Hachette UK's policy is to use papers that are natural, renewable and recyclable products and made from wood grown in sustainable forests. The logging and manufacturing processes are expected to conform to the environmental regulations of the country of origin.

P1972

Get the most from this book

Everyone has to decide his or her own revision strategy, but it is essential to review your work, learn it and test your understanding. These Revision Notes will help you to do that in a planned way, topic by topic. Use this book as the cornerstone of your revision and don't hesitate to write in it — personalise your notes and check your progress by ticking off each section as you revise.

☑ Tick to track your progress

Use the revision planner on page 4 to plan your revision, topic by topic. Tick each box when you have:

● revised and understood a topic

● tested yourself

● practised the exam questions and gone online to check your answers and complete the quick quizzes

You can also keep track of your revision by ticking off each topic heading in the book. You may find it helpful to add your own notes as you work through each topic.

My revision planner ☑

Unit 1 People and politics

	Revised	Tested	Gone online
1 Democracy and political participation			
7 Nature of democracy	☐	☐	☐
11 Democracy in the UK	☐	☐	☐
14 Enhancing democracy	☐	☐	☐

Role of the prime minister and cabinet

Nature of the cabinet ———— Revised ☐

The cabinet in the UK has the following characteristics:

● It is composed of 20–25 senior politicians, all appointed directly by the prime minister.

● Members of the cabinet must be members of either the House of Commons (i.e. they are MPs) or the House of Lords (i.e. peers). If the

Features to help you succeed

Examiner's tips and summaries

Throughout the book there are tips from the examiner to help you boost your final grade.

Summaries provide advice on how to approach each topic in the exams, and suggest other things you might want to mention to gain those valuable extra marks.

Definitions and key words

Clear, concise definitions of essential key terms are provided on the page where they appear.

Key words from the specification are highlighted in bold for you throughout the book.

Typical mistakes

The examiner identifies the typical mistakes candidates make and explains how you can avoid them.

Now test yourself

These short, knowledge-based questions provide the first step in testing your learning. Answers are at the back of the book.

Check your understanding

Use these questions at the end of each section to make sure that you have understood every topic. Answers are at the back of the book

Exam practice

Practice exam questions are provided for each topic. Use them to consolidate your revision and practise your exam skills.

Online

Go online to check and print out your answers to the exam questions and try out the extra quick quizzes at **www.therevisionbutton.co.uk/myrevisionnotes**

My revision planner

Exam practice answers and quick quizzes at **www.therevisionbutton.co.uk/myrevisionnotes**

Countdown to my exams

6–8 weeks to go

- Start by looking at the specification — make sure you know exactly what material you need to revise and the style of the examination. Use the revision planner on page 4 to familiarise yourself with the topics.
- Organise your notes, making sure you have covered everything on the specification. The revision planner will help you to group your notes into topics.
- Work out a realistic revision plan that will allow you time for relaxation. Set aside days and times for all the subjects that you need to study, and stick to your timetable.
- Set yourself sensible targets. Break your revision down into focused sessions of around 40 minutes, divided by breaks. These Revision Notes organise the basic facts into short, memorable sections to make revising easier.

Revised ☐

4–6 weeks to go

- Read through the relevant sections of this book and refer to the examiner's tips, examiner's summaries, typical mistakes and key terms. Tick off the topics as you feel confident about them. Highlight those topics you find difficult and look at them again in detail.
- Test your understanding of each topic by working through the 'Now test yourself' and 'Check your understanding' questions in the book. Look up the answers at the back of the book.
- Make a note of any problem areas as you revise, and ask your teacher to go over these in class.
- Look at past papers. They are one of the best ways to revise and practise your exam skills. Write or prepare planned answers to the exam practice questions provided in this book. Check your answers online and try out the extra quick quizzes at **www.therevisionbutton.co.uk/ myrevisionnotes**
- Try different revision methods. For example, you can make notes using mind maps, spider diagrams or flash cards.
- Track your progress using the revision planner and give yourself a reward when you have achieved your target.

Revised ☐

One week to go

- Try to fit in at least one more timed practice of an entire past paper and seek feedback from your teacher, comparing your work closely with the mark scheme.
- Check the revision planner to make sure you haven't missed out any topics. Brush up on any areas of difficulty by talking them over with a friend or getting help from your teacher.
- Attend any revision classes put on by your teacher. Remember, he or she is an expert at preparing people for examinations.

Revised ☐

The day before the examination

- Flick through these Revision Notes for useful reminders, for example the examiner's tips, examiner's summaries, typical mistakes and key terms.
- Check the time and place of your examination.
- Make sure you have everything you need — extra pens and pencils, tissues, a watch, bottled water, sweets.
- Allow some time to relax and have an early night to ensure you are fresh and alert for the examinations.

Revised ☐

My exams

AS UK Government & Politics Unit 1

Date: ....

Time: ....

Location: ....

AS UK Government & Politics Unit 2

Date: ....

Time: ....

Location: ....

1 Democracy and political participation

There are three main elements to the knowledge required in this section. The first is to be able to define and explain certain democratic principles, such as legitimacy, representation and participation. Such knowledge also requires you to make some key distinctions between different elements of democracy. The second is to know and be able to analyse various democratic elements and processes. The third is to be able to evaluate a number of proposed changes to democracy in the UK as well as the extent to which the UK conforms to various democratic features.

Nature of democracy

What is legitimacy? Revised

Legitimacy means in general the 'right to govern' and to 'make laws' which will be enforced and are likely to be obeyed by the people. In more detail:

- A regime may be legitimate because its government is widely recognised. However, the legitimacy of some regimes may be disputed.

  Example: The government of the UK is universally recognised whereas the legitimacy of the government of Kosovo is disputed.

  > **Legitimacy** refers to the right of an individual or body to be recognised and to have the right to exercise power. In democratic countries, legitimacy is normally conveyed by election.

- Legitimacy can refer to the degree to which a body or a government can be justified in exercising **power**.

  Example: Are the House of Lords and the monarchy legitimate in the UK, given that neither is elected?

  > **Power** refers to the ability of an individual or a body to force others to do something they might otherwise not do. Power is normally said to have three levels:
  > - coercion, which means force, often physical force
  > - political power, which involves the use of rewards and sanctions, legal authority and persuasion
  > - influence, which means being able to affect how others act or think, but no force is involved

- In the democratic world, legitimacy is normally conferred by election. It could be argued that British government lacks legitimacy as it is elected on a minority of the national vote.

  Example: It could be argued that the 2010 coalition lacked legitimacy because it did not have an electoral mandate.

Legitimacy is closely related to the concept of **authority**.

Authority, like legitimacy, means the 'right to exercise power'. It is usually said to derive from three possible sources:
- tradition — because power has been exercised for a long time and has been accepted for many years
- election — power may be exercised if an individual or party has been elected
- charisma — a person develops authority through the force of their personality and their ability to inspire a following

What is consent and how can it be recognised?

Revised

Consent in politics refers to evidence that the people consent to be governed in a particular way and/or by a particular government. Consent can be conferred in these ways:
- by free elections
- by good turnouts in free elections
- by a distinct lack of popular dissent
- by clear demonstrations of support for government
- by an explicit referendum (also known as a plebiscite) to adopt a particular constitution

The presence of these factors is evidence of consent.

Examiner's tip

Consent and legitimacy are difficult concepts. Examiners will be looking both for a short, precise definition and for some elaboration of the definition. Elaboration will normally involve explanations of why they are difficult concepts and why their meaning may be uncertain: for example, 'Consent means that the people support or will tolerate the system of government of a country. Low turnouts at election may be evidence of lack of consent, but not necessarily. Lack of dissent may be stronger evidence of the existence of consent.'

What is citizenship?

Revised

- The status of being a citizen grants a person the enjoyment of certain rights.

  Example: In a democracy these are the right to vote, to stand for office, to be granted a fair trial if accused of a crime, to be treated equally by the law and to be guaranteed justice.

- Citizenship also implies the enjoyment of civil liberties.

  Example: freedom of expression, of movement, of thought, of association.

- Citizenship also carries certain duties or obligations.

  Example: to obey the law, to pay taxes, possibly to defend the country.

- The modern idea of 'active citizenship', developed by Labour in the 1990s and followed by the Conservatives after 2010 in their 'Big Society' programme, is that as citizens we also have a duty to be politically active.

  Example: volunteering for charity work, environmental protection, being politically active and socially responsible.

What is democracy? —

General definition: any system of government where the people have access to independent information and are able to influence government decisions. It also implies that government makes itself accountable to the people. Democracy can take a number of forms, the main two being direct and representative democracy.

Features of a modern democracy

A modern democracy has the following features:

- There is a peaceful transition of power from one government to the next.
- There are free and fair regular elections.
- People have open access to independent information, including free press and other media.
- Government should be accountable to the people and representative institutions.
- There is a high degree of freedom for individuals and groups.
- Different political ideologies and beliefs are tolerated.
- The rule of law applies — all are equal under the law.
- Government operates in the broad interests of the people.

> **Examples:** UK, USA, France.

> **Typical mistake**
>
> It is an error to believe that there is one 'perfect' form of democracy. This is not true. Democracy can have a number of variations, but can be accurately described as 'democracy' if it conforms to the definition given here.

What is direct democracy? —

In direct democracy:

- People themselves make decisions, usually through referendums.
- People are directly consulted on political decisions — this is also known as *consultative democracy*.
- People may take the initiative in creating political change (i.e. popular action provokes a political decision).

> **Examples:** referendums (UK, on AV in May 2011), initiatives (USA and Switzerland), public consultations (English local government).

What is representative democracy? —

In representative democracy:

- The people elect representatives.
- The people do not make most decisions themselves, but delegate that power to their representatives.
- There are political parties that represent different political views.
- Associations and pressure groups represent different sections of society, interests and causes.
- There are representative assemblies that express the will of the people and of sections of society.

representation

'Burkean' representation, named after the conservative philosopher Edmund Burke, states that elected representatives should use their own judgement rather than slavishly following the wishes of their constituency or party.

Delegation is the idea that a representative should follow very closely the wishes of those who have elected him or her.

Party representation means that if a representative is a member of a party, they are expected to support and vote for the known policies of that party.

How representation operates in the UK
Revised

In the UK:

- Representation operates through MPs — they represent individual constituents, whole constituencies, sometimes sectional interests, sometimes causes, sometimes the national interest.
- Most MPs, however, represent their party and its electoral manifesto.
- Parties have a representative function. They represent both sections of society and particular political views.
- Pressure groups represent interests and causes.
- The House of Commons as a whole can represent the national interest.
- The House of Lords is a vehicle for representation as many peers represent sections of society and prominent causes as well as the national interest.

Parliamentary democracy is a form of liberal democracy in which a parliament or elected assembly is the key institution. It means that parliament is the source of political power. It also means that parliament makes government accountable and government is a part of parliament. It implies that parliament is the main vehicle for representation. Government is also drawn from parliament.

Examiner's tip

Examiners like to see practical examples of representation: for example, cases where a specific MP has represented his or her constituency, or where a section of society has been effectively represented in the House of Lords and/or by a pressure group.

Typical mistake

Don't forget that pressure groups are a key aspect of representative democracy today. The difference between pressure groups and other forms of representation is that pressure groups are not formal and may not be part of any institution.

Now test yourself
Tested

1 Copy this table and fill in the right-hand column to illustrate how the various institutions are representative in nature.

Institution	How the institutions can be said to be representative
MPs	
House of Commons	
House of Lords	
Political parties	
Pressure groups	

Answers on p. 103

Exam practice answers and quick quizzes at **www.therevisionbutton.co.uk/myrevisionnotes**

What is pluralist democracy?

Revised

In pluralist democracy:

- Multiple parties and political associations are allowed to operate.
- Different political beliefs are tolerated and allowed to flourish.
- There are many sources of independent information and opinion through the media.
- Power is dispersed among different individuals, bodies and institutions, rather than being concentrated in one or a few locations.

> **Example:** USA.

What is a liberal democracy?

Revised

A liberal democracy has all the general features of democracy (see above). In addition:

- Individual liberties are respected and well protected.
- There is a strong constitution that limits the powers of government.
- Government features strong internal checks and balances.
- There is a high level of political toleration.

> **Example:** Germany.

Typical mistake

Some students make the mistake of believing that liberal democracy refers to 'democracy as liberals define it'. Though this is not strictly wrong, liberal democracy is a term that is now widely accepted in the democratic world.

Democracy in the UK

The UK's political system combines elements of representative and direct democracy.

Advantages of representative democracy

Revised

Representative democracy has the following advantages:

- Most people do not have the time to be continually involved in politics, so they can elect representatives to act on their behalf.
- Representatives may have more experience, knowledge and expertise than the rest of the population.
- Representatives can be made accountable for their decisions, whereas the people as a whole cannot.
- The demands of the people may be incoherent and contradictory. Representatives can 'aggregate' — that is, convert incoherent demands into coherent political programmes.
- People can react emotionally to issues. Representatives can be more rational.
- Representatives can educate the public about political issues.
- Different sections of society and various political causes and beliefs can be well represented by elected representatives.

> **Examples:** MPs in the UK, US congressmen, pressure group influence on the EU, party politics.

Advantages of direct democracy and referendums

Direct democracy also has many benefits:

- It is the purest form of democracy, dating back to ancient Athens.
- Important decisions can be strengthened if they receive the direct consent of the people. Referendums give decisions legitimacy.
- Referendums and direct consultation can educate the public about political issues.
- People can participate more directly in direct democracy. This improves engagement with politics and may strengthen positive citizenship.
- Important constitutional changes can be 'entrenched' through a referendum.
- When government itself is divided, referendums can solve the conflict and secure a consensus decision.

> **Examples:** referendums on British membership of the EU in 1975, referendums on devolution in 1997 and the referendum on AV in 2011.

> In a **referendum** the people are invited, on a national, regional or local basis, to vote on a key political issue, usually of a constitutional nature. Referendums pose a simple question which requires a straight-forward 'yes' or 'no' answer. In the UK referendum results are not legally binding, but Parliament will, effectively, always accept a referendum result.

Disadvantages of representative democracy

Representative democracy is subject to the following disadvantages:

- It may be difficult to make representatives accountable between elections.
- Representatives may ignore or distort the demands of the people to suit their own political advantage.
- When dominated by parties, representatives may follow the party line rather than represent their constituents accurately.
- Representative democracy may result in too much political conflict which can only be resolved by direct democracy.
- The idea of the electoral mandate is flawed in that voters are only presented with a manifesto, the whole of which they must either accept or reject. Voters cannot express preferences within various election manifestos.

> **Examples:** problems presented by the 2010 British coalition; low electoral turnouts in the UK after 2001 suggest loss of faith in party politics.

Disadvantages of direct democracy and referendums

Direct democracy also has its problems:

- Issues may be too complex for the average person to understand.

> **Example:** British membership of the European single currency.

- People may vote in an emotional, irrational way.

> **Example:** a vote on capital punishment.

- If there are too many referendums, people may suffer from 'voter fatigue' and so the turnout may be low.

Exam practice answers and quick quizzes at **www.therevisionbutton.co.uk/myrevisionnotes**

- Voters may start to lose respect for representative institutions if they become used to making their own decisions.
- Referendums and direct democracy may encourage the 'tyranny of the majority', which results in the oppression of minorities.

> **Example:** the 2009 Swiss referendum banning the construction of Islamic minarets, a vote in California in 2008 outlawing civil partnerships.

- If there is a low turnout in a referendum, the result may lack legitimacy.

> **Example:** only 34% turnout in referendum to decide whether London should have an elected mayor, 1998.

- A very close referendum vote may result in an unsatisfactory conclusion and fail to achieve acceptance of the outcome.

> **Example:** the vote for Welsh devolution in 1997 was Yes — 50.5%, No — 49.5%.

The use of referendums in the UK — Revised

> **Example 1:** When the government is split on an issue, a referendum will resolve that issue without destroying government itself:

- 1975: referendum on whether or not the UK should remain in the European Community. Result: 'Yes'.
- 2011: referendum on whether to adopt AV as an electoral system. Result: 'No'.

> **Example 2:** When an important constitutional change is being proposed which will affect the way people are governed:

- 1998: referendum in London on whether to adopt an elected mayor. Result: 'Yes'.
- 2004: referendum in northeast England on whether to introduce an elected regional assembly. Result: 'No'.

> **Example 3:** When it is necessary to entrench an important constitutional change:

- 1997: referendum on whether to introduce devolved government in Scotland. Result: 'Yes'.
- 1997: referendum on whether to give the Scottish Parliament the power to vary the level of income tax. Result: 'Yes'.
- 1997: referendum on whether to introduce an assembly in Wales. Result: 'Yes'.

> **Example 4:** When there is a special need to secure popular consent:

- 1998: referendum in Northern Ireland to approve the Belfast (Good Friday) Agreement designed to introduce devolved government and end inter-community conflict. Result: 'Yes'.

> **Examiner's tip**
>
> Examiners want to see plenty of accurate examples. In the case of referendums they are looking for important examples of referendums together with clear explanations of *why* they were held. Slight errors of fact (e.g. a date a year or two out) are not so important, but the basic facts of a referendum should be correct.

Comparing direct and representative democracy — Revised

The following distinctions can be drawn between representative and direct democracy:

- Direct democracy is purer than representative democracy.

- Direct democracy tends to operate in connection with constitutional changes and reforms, whereas representative democracy concerns the day-to-day, year-to-year running of the country.
- Representative democracy considers various different interests in society and is more pluralistic, whereas direct democracy represents only the will of the majority.
- Representatives are accountable for their decisions while the people cannot be accountable to themselves.
- Referendums can be seen as more legitimate than decisions made by representative institutions.

Now test yourself

Tested

2 In the table below, fill in the middle column to show examples of referendums used for each of the reasons given. In the third column, fill in the outcome.

Why the referendum was necessary	Example(s) of such a referendum	Outcome
To achieve popular consent to a constitutional change.		
The government itself was divided on the issue.		
It was necessary to achieve widespread consent for a specific reason.		
To entrench an important constitutional change, preventing it from being overturned by a future parliament.		

Answers on p. 103

Enhancing democracy

Participation in UK politics

Revised

In the UK, citizens can participate in the democratic process by:
- voting in local, regional and national elections
- voting in referendums
- taking part in political consultation exercises
- being a member and supporter of a pressure group
- being a pressure group activist
- joining a political party
- becoming an activist in a political party (member of local party committees, canvassing, etc.)
- standing for public office at local, regional or national level

Evidence of a decline in political participation

Revised

There is considerable evidence of a decline in participation in the UK:
- Turnouts in national and regional elections have been falling (see Table 1.1).

- Turnouts in referendums tend to be low.
- Party membership has been falling since the 1980s.
- Activism in political parties has fallen.
- There is evidence of widespread disillusionment with party politics.
- Identification with parties has fallen.

Table 1.1 UK election turnouts (%)

General election		
1992		77.7
1997		71.4
2001		59.4
2005		61.4
2010		65.1
Scottish Parliamentary elections		
1999		59.1
2003		49.4
2007		51.8
2011		51.2
Referendums		
1975	Membership of European Community	64.5
1997	Devolution of power to Scotland	60.4
1997	Devolution of power to Wales	50.1
1998	Northern Ireland Good Friday Agreement	81.0
1998	Elected mayor in London	34.1
2011	AV electoral system	42.2

Typical mistake

Although there has certainly been a significant decline in political participation in the UK, it is a mistake to assume this is the only trend. In some areas, such as pressure group membership and direct action, participation is actually increasing.

Methods of increasing political participation

Revised

Several methods have been suggested for increasing participation, each of which has pros and cons.

Compulsory voting

Arguments for:

- It increases turnout.
- It forces people to think about politics.
- People become more used to voting.
- Results have more legitimacy and thus are respected.

Arguments against:

- It abuses people's freedom.
- Results may be seen as artificial.
- It is costly to enforce.
- It cannot solve the problem of apathy.

Votes at 16

Arguments for:

- It makes the young politically aware.
- It improves the level of identification with politics.
- It makes political education more relevant.

Arguments against:

- 16-year-olds are too young to make a judgement.
- Many 16-year-olds may not vote.
- There may be a distortion of party policies to attract young voters.

Citizenship education

Arguments for:

- It improves political knowledge.
- It encourages engagement with politics.

Arguments against:

- Education is expensive.
- It may not create genuine interest.

E-democracy (digital democracy)

Arguments for:

- It provides greater access to politics for citizens.
- It can promote a more direct form of democracy.
- E-voting might increase electoral turnout.
- The internet provides a vast source of independent political information.

Arguments against:

- It is vulnerable to fraud and hacking.
- Illicit and false information can circulate easily.
- Those who lack technical knowledge might be excluded.

Evidence of increasing political participation

Revised

It can be argued that political participation is increasing in some ways.

Pressure groups are growing in number and membership.

> **Examples:** environmental groups, old age campaigners.

There is increasing use of campaigning through the social media.

> **Examples:** campaigns against road pricing, against sale of National Forest

There has been a growth in examples of direct action.

> **Examples:** anti-tuition fees campaign, anti-Iraq war campaign.

Exam practice answers and quick quizzes at **www.therevisionbutton.co.uk/myrevisionnotes**

How democratic is the UK?

Positives

- There are regular, free elections.
- There are free media and many independent sources of political information.
- There are democratic institutions, notably local councils, devolved assemblies, Parliament and government.
- There is freedom to vote, to stand for office and to form political parties or other political associations.
- Parliament makes government continually accountable for its actions.
- Referendums are held from time to time when important constitutional issues are to be resolved.
- A variety of parties and political associations such as pressure groups are allowed to flourish.
- Freedom, equality and rights are protected by the European Convention on Human Rights, by parliamentary statutes and by common law.
- There is an independent judiciary that safeguards the rule of law.
- The rule of law apples — all are equal under the law.
- The Freedom of Information Act enables citizens to access important information about government and the administration of the state.

Negatives

- Unelected institutions persist in the form of the monarchy and the House of Lords.
- Elections are arguably not fair owing to the first-past-the-post system.
- Governments are elected on a minority of the national vote.
- The prime minister enjoys arbitrary, prerogative powers.
- There is no entrenched constitution, so the distribution of political power is often uncertain.
- Parliamentary sovereignty means that individual rights and liberties are inadequately protected.
- A great deal of power has been transferred to the European Union, which has weaker democratic institutions.
- Arguably, political participation is declining.
- There is a growing degree of political disengagement.

> **Typical mistake**
>
> Don't be too narrow in discussing only institutions, such as the House of Lords and the electoral system. You should also include broader problems of the UK's democracy, such as low election turnouts and general 'disengagement' with parties and politics.

Now test yourself

3 Some aspects of the decline in political participation are listed below. In each case, give a proposed solution to the problem, explaining briefly why it may be a solution.

(a) There is widespread disillusionment and lack of respect for politicians in general.

(b) People feel excluded from political decision making.

(c) There is widespread ignorance of political issues.

(d) Turnout at elections is low.

Answers on p. 103

Assessment of methods of improving UK democracy

Various suggestions have been made for improving democracy in the UK. These are critically assessed below.

Replacing the monarchy with an elected head of state

Arguments for:

- This would increase the democratic legitimacy of the head of state.
- It would make the head of state democratically accountable.
- An elected head of state would be able to settle political deadlocks.
- An elected head of state could increase popular political engagement.

Arguments against:

- A political head of state might destabilise politics.
- Such a head of state might give too much power to the governing party.
- The UK would lose an important historical institution.

Introducing an elected second chamber

Arguments for:

- This would increase the legitimacy of the second chamber.
- A democratic second chamber would be an effective check on government power.

Arguments against:

- An elected second chamber might be less independent.
- It might check government excessively.
- It might challenge the authority of the Commons.

Reforming the electoral system

Arguments for:

- Alternative systems would be fairer and give the electorate more real choices, reducing the numbers of wasted votes.
- The House of Commons would be more politically representative.
- It would increase the democratic legitimacy of MPs and government.
- The outcome would probably reflect the pluralistic nature of politics more accurately.

Arguments against:

- Proportional representation would remove the important MP–constituency link.
- Multiparty government might ensue and be less stable. It would be more difficult to form a government if no party won an overall majority.
- There would be unpredictable consequences.
- Voters might find it difficult to accept a new system.

Exam practice answers and quick quizzes at **www.therevisionbutton.co.uk/myrevisionnotes**

Increased use of referendums

Arguments for:

- Referendums would increase political awareness.
- They could be seen as a purer form of democracy.
- They would improve political 'education'.
- They would increase political participation.

Arguments against:

- Too many votes might result in 'voter fatigue' and low turnouts.
- The electorate might find many issues too complex to understand properly.
- Referendums could lead to the 'tyranny of the majority'. Minorities might be discriminated against.
- Voters might be unduly influenced by emotional, irrational appeals.
- Voters might lose respect for representative institutions and for political processes in general.

Introducing a codified constitution

Arguments for:

- A written constitution might stop the drift towards excessive power of government and the prime minister.
- It would make citizens more aware of how the political system works.
- It might create more public engagement with the political system.
- Rights and freedoms would be better protected.

Arguments against:

- The political system would lose its flexibility.
- It would destroy many political traditions and so reduce public attachment to politics.
- It might put too much power into the hands of unelected, unaccountable judges who have to interpret a constitution.

Decentralising the political system

Arguments for:

- Local and regional government are smaller scale and seen as more democratic.
- Government would be less 'remote', and closer to the people.
- There might be less tight party control over politics.
- It would strengthen local communities.
- The growing power of central government would be curbed.

Arguments against:

- More powerful local and regional government would mean more variable state provision.
- Citizens might take local and regional government less seriously, resulting in, for example, low voting turnouts.
- Tensions between central and decentralised government might increase.

> **Examiner's tip**
>
> The examiners will often be looking for evaluation, not just descriptions. So, for example, you will need to describe ways of improving democracy, but if the question demands it, you should also provide a balanced evaluation of how effective they are likely to be and/or whether they are desirable.

Check your understanding

1 What is direct democracy?
2 What is representative democracy?
3 Distinguish between direct and representative democracy.
4 What is a referendum?
5 Describe two examples of referendums.
6 Give three ways in which people participate in politics.
7 Define 'liberal democracy'.

Answers on p. 103

Exam practice

Part (a) questions

1 What is democracy?   [5]
2 Outline three ways in which people are represented in the UK.   [5]
3 What is meant by 'pluralist democracy'?   [5]
4 Outline the circumstances of any two referendums held in the UK.   [5]

Part (b) questions

5 Explain the main ways in which people are represented in the UK.   [10]
6 Assess the case for using referendums to determine important political issues.   [10]
7 Assess any three ways of increasing participation in UK politics.   [10]
8 Explain three ways in which the British political system may be seen as undemocratic. [10]

Part (c) questions

9 To what extent can the UK be said to be a liberal democracy?   [25]
10 Why have referendums been held in the UK?   [25]
11 Explain the democratic deficit and ways in which it could it be eliminated.   [25]
12 How and to what extent is representative democracy superior to direct democracy? [25]

Answers and quick quiz 1 online

Examiner's summary

✔ There are a number of different conceptions of types of democracy. Examiners will often ask about these, requiring candidates to describe them and to illustrate with examples.

✔ The UK political system should be evaluated in terms of how democratic it is. Examiners will expect a critical assessment of various aspects of democracy in the UK.

✔ Students must have a thorough knowledge of the theory, use and results of referendums. These should be combined with a critical evaluation of referendums. Several examples of the use of referendums must be known and used.

✔ Knowledge of how democracy and participation in the UK can be improved will be required, but any proposals must also be critically assessed, pointing out their strengths and weaknesses.

✔ A common error is to assume that low election turnouts and falling party membership are proof that democratic participation is in long-term decline. People can participate in many ways, other than voting and party activism.

✔ A second typical shortcoming occurs when discussing referendums. Students should know both why referendums were held (i.e. why the issue was not resolved by Parliament) and the nature of the issue in question.

2 Party policies and ideas

Political parties are the key to understanding the British political system. The parties are the main developers of policy, they are the main breeding ground for aspiring politicians and they have a major representative role. The basic ideals of the parties and their current policies are, therefore, crucial to understanding the political process. Party ideas are constantly evolving and many examination questions focus on such changes.

Nature of political parties

What are the main features of political parties? — Revised

- Each party consists of a group of individuals who have a commonly held ideology and a shared set of principles or values.
- They are united by ideas and values, and wish to promote these and manage the country according to them.
- They normally have a formal organisation with a leadership, active members and a mass membership.
- They have mechanisms for developing policy, selecting candidates for office and identifying leaders.

> A **political party** is an association of people who hold similar political views and who have the goal of implementing those views by becoming a government or sharing in government.

What are the main functions of political parties? — Revised

The principal functions of political parties are as follows:

- They aggregate ideas and put together a comprehensive and coherent set of policy options which are based on their political principles. They convert these policies into a workable political programme of action.
- They contest elections. In this process they set out their ideas in a manifesto. A manifesto is a statement of policies and intentions.
- They select appropriate people to stand for election to local councils, to devolved assemblies in Scotland, Wales, Northern Ireland and Greater London, and to the UK Parliament.
- They provide the personnel of government. If a political party wins a general election, the victorious party appoints its leading members to government.
- They provide representation and speak up for various sections of the community.
- They provide political education to the general public concerning which options the country should take.

> **Examiner's tip**
>
> When discussing the roles of parties, remember that examiners are especially interested in those roles that enhance democracy, such as educating and informing the public and providing opportunities for political participation.

Now test yourself

1   List three of the main functions of political parties. In each case, describe the ways in which those functions or roles enhance a liberal democracy.

Answers on p. 104

Differences between left-wing and right-wing ideas

Revised

The terms 'left wing' and 'right wing' are often used in relation to modern politics. They are slightly vague ideas and can be misleading. However, the following descriptions can safely be used in examination answers.

The political left

The 'left' is characterised by the following ideas:

- Collectivism, which is a belief that goals can be achieved by collective action as well as by the efforts of individuals. This includes the idea of the state as an essential and positive force in the lives of all.
- A belief that the interests of the wider community are often superior to the interests of individuals.
- A belief in the universal distribution of benefits such as health, education and social insurance.
- A positive view of human nature and a belief that human beings are essentially social animals, rather than self-seeking individuals.
- Support for equality, fraternity and maximum freedom.

Example: Socialism is a clear example of a left-wing political philosophy.

The political right

The 'right' is characterised by the following ideas:

- A firm belief in the importance of the individual and the expression of individual choice.
- A belief that individuals have a flawed human nature and therefore need discipline.
- Disagreement with collectivism.
- A view that the role of the state in people's lives should be limited.
- A view of human nature suggesting that individuals prefer to pursue their own goals and may see their own interests as more important than those of the wider community.
- A belief that inequality and differences in living standards can be a positive force, creating incentives for individuals to improve themselves and not rely on the state.
- A view that the peace and security of the community is more important than the rights and freedoms of individuals.

Examples: Traditional and 'New Right' conservatism are clear examples of right-wing political philosophies.

> **Left/right wing** is a way of dividing political ideas into two tendencies. Left-wing ideas are associated with a tendency towards socialism and involve such beliefs as collectivism, equality and social justice. Right-wing ideas are most associated with conservatism and include ideas such as a belief in free markets, nationalism, a strong position on law and order, and support for tradition.

Tested

Now test yourself

2   Study the following policies and ideas. In each case, tick the appropriate column to indicate whether they are right-wing or left-wing ideas.

Idea	Left-wing idea	Right-wing idea
1 The redistribution of real income from rich to poor through tax policies		
2 The bringing of major industries under state control		
3 A belief in free markets and low taxation		
4 Opposition to strong trade unions		
5 Strong support for the welfare state		
6 A hard line on crime, law and order		

Answers on p. 104

What are consensus and adversary politics?

Revised

Consensus means:

● general agreement between the parties within a particular policy area

● a period of politics when there are wide areas of agreement on key issues

● an agreement between parties not to engage in political conflict on an issue because there is an overwhelming need for unity: for example, in times of war

Adversary politics means:

● a high degree of ideological conflict between the main parties

● few areas of agreement between the parties

In 2011, three main areas of consensus politics were as follows:

● There is an overwhelming need to reduce harmful emissions which cause climate change.

● British involvement in the Afghanistan conflict is justified.

● There is a need to bring down the huge government financial deficit, although parties differ on how quickly this should be done.

In 2011, three main areas of adversary politics were:

● whether there needs to be extensive reform of the NHS

● how to deal with the high levels of crime and the growing prison population

● whether the ability of trade unions to call strikes should be curtailed

Consensus politics refers to a high degree of political agreement between and within parties over a range of political issues.

Adversary politics refers to a situation where there is a great deal of policy conflict between and within parties. There are key ideological splits within the political community.

Typical mistake

There is often confusion between 'adversary' politics and 'adversarial' politics. The first refers to there being wide differences between parties in terms of ideologies and policies. Adversarial politics, on the other hand, is a *style* of politics involving a great deal of argument and aggression. You will not be asked about adversarial politics.

Traditions and policies of parties

Traditions of the Conservative Party

There are two main conservative traditions. The first is usually known as **traditional conservatism** and has developed since the nineteenth century. The other is normally known as the **'New Right'** or 'Thatcherism'. It developed during the 1980s.

Traditional conservatism

The main traditional conservative ideas are summarised in Table 2.1.

> **Conservatism** is a political tendency which developed largely in the nineteenth century. It implies a belief in order and security, and opposition to ideologies such as socialism and extreme liberalism. It also suggests a traditional and pragmatic approach to political issues, with some suspicion of radical change.

Table 2.1 Traditional conservative beliefs

Ideas and principles	Examples of ideas and principles reflected in practical policies
Order. Traditional conservatives believe that order in society is a strong human need. Without good order, progress cannot be achieved.	• Strong authoritarian policies on law and order. • Taking a hard line against organised protest in society. • A general belief in strong government.
Organic society. This is a twofold philosophy. First, society is like a living organism and should be allowed to develop naturally, without artificial intervention. Secondly, all the sections of society depend on each other and are part of a single whole. We are not merely free individuals.	• Parties and governments should not seek to impose their own beliefs upon society. • Policies should be aimed at maintaining a strong, united society.
Fear of diversity. The belief in an organic society leads to a fear of too much social and cultural diversity, which might threaten social unity.	• Opposition to multiculturalism. • Resistance to large amounts of immigration. • Intolerance towards 'unconventional lifestyles'.
Support for tradition. Conservatives believe that traditions are important in maintaining unity, and continuity with the past. They provide a means by which a society can unite around common institutions and values. Traditions refer to both institutions and values.	• Opposition to reforms that threaten traditional institutions, such as electoral reform, reform of the House of Lords, a changed role for the monarchy or movement towards a codified constitution. • Strong support for traditional values, largely surrounding the traditional family and traditional morality. As far as possible the state should support these values through its policies.
Support for private property and accumulated wealth. Conservatives see the ownership of property and wealth as being important in two ways. First, they are an expression of a family's individualism and their aspirations. Secondly, those who enjoy property and wealth have a greater sense of responsibility. Wealthy people have a responsibility to help those less fortunate. This last doctrine is known as *noblesse oblige*.	• Taxes on property and wealth should be held down and possibly eliminated. • The rights of property owners should be protected, notably through strong policies on law and order and privacy laws. • Conservatives have supported the idea that the wealthy should support the less privileged, but largely through the voluntary sector rather than high taxation.
Pragmatism. It is a principle of conservatism that each problem in government should be dealt with on its own merits and not according to any fixed doctrines or ideology. Thus conservatives have opposed socialism and liberalism as such fixed doctrines.	• Policies to be judged on their merits. Those which seem to favour the public good should be retained and those which do not, rejected, no matter whether they come from left- or right-wing ideas. • In foreign policy the UK's national interest should always be pursued.

'New Right' conservatism or Thatcherism

The main New Right ideas are summarised in Table 2.2.

Table 2.2 The New Right Under Margaret Thatcher

Ideas and principles	Examples of ideas and principles reflected in practical policies
The free market and neoliberalism. Margaret Thatcher and her leadership group were 'neoliberals'. They believed that, wherever possible, markets should be free from intervention or interference by government, trade unions or large, powerful corporations. The solution to virtually all economic problems lay in free markets correcting themselves automatically. This meant free markets for products, finance and labour.	• Most large, nationalised (publicly owned and state-run) industries were sold off into private hands. These included gas, electricity, water, telecommunications, steel, coal and railways (railways were privatised very late, in 1996). • Some industries were made open to competition and monopolies were broken up. These included the professions (law, opticians, etc.). The financial markets were made more open and competitive, and banks were allowed to compete with building societies. • State-run services were opened up to competition between the state itself and private companies.
Anti-unionism. The New Right believed that powerful trade unions were a barrier to economic progress. They prevented labour markets being flexible, forced wages up too high and prevented technological progress in many industries.	• The legal powers of trade unions were severely reduced. • Unions were forced to make themselves more internally democratic to break up unaccountable leadership groups. • The ability of unions to take industrial action to further their aims was reduced.
Low direct taxation. New Right conservatives saw direct taxes on individuals and private companies as a disincentive to work and enterprise.	• Income tax levels were reduced, especially at higher earning levels. The revenue was made up by higher indirect taxes such as VAT. • Taxes on private company profits were reduced.
State disengagement from economic management. As neoliberals, these conservatives believed that economic problems would solve themselves in the medium term, as long as governments resisted the temptation to try to manage the economy. The only justifiable intervention was in controlling the total amount of money in circulation (the money supply) to prevent inflation. This policy was known as monetarism.	• Government did not intervene when there were economic slumps in the early 1980s and 1990s. • Government controlled money supply tightly.
Dependency culture. Thatcherite conservatives saw excessively high levels of welfare benefits as a disincentive to work, enterprise and self-reliance. This created a 'dependency culture' where people became used to relying on state support.	• Many welfare benefits were reduced or eliminated. • Benefits were targeted on those in most need, and who were unable to be self-reliant through no fault of their own.
Neoconservatism. Recognising that a much freer society could create the danger of disorder and moral decline, the New Right adopted American neoconservative ideals. These included a strong position on law and order and attempts to maintain traditional, Christian morality. Substantial cultural diversity was discouraged.	• Strong policing policies, including greater powers to control demonstrations and public disorder. • Longer, more severe sentences for criminals. • Support for the institution of traditional marriage.
Property. Like traditional conservatives, the New Right emphasised the importance of home ownership.	• Tenants in local authority housing were given the right to buy their homes at discounted prices and mortgage rates. • The markets supplying mortgages were opened up to greater competition and it was made easier for families to obtain mortgages and other credit.

Typical mistake

The term 'neoliberalism' is often applied to New Right, Thatcherite conservatism. It means a belief in free markets and economic freedom. However, neoliberalism is a right-wing tendency and it is a mistake to think of it as part of mainstream liberalism.

Comparing New Right and traditional conservatism

So how do New Right and traditional conservatism differ?

Differences

The main distinctions can be summarised as follows:

- Traditional conservatives see society as organic whereas the New Rights see society as merely a collection of individuals. Margaret Thatcher famously stated, 'There is no such thing as society.'
- Traditional conservatives support free markets but take a pragmatic view of economic management, believing that there are times when state intervention is needed. The New Right is ideologically opposed to state intervention.
- Traditional conservatives have favoured a mixed economy, with some key industries remaining under state control. The New Rights have been determined virtually to eliminate state control of industry and commerce.
- Traditional conservatives are more supportive of the welfare state than the New Right.
- While traditional conservatives take a pragmatic view of policies generally, judging each case on its merits, the New Right is more ideological and tended to govern on the basis of its fixed ideas.

Similarities

The main similarities can be summarised as follows:

- Both strands of conservatism take an authoritarian view of law and order issues.
- Both support traditional Christian, family and 'British' values.
- Both have an instinct for free markets and low taxation, although the New Right are more dogmatic about these principles, while traditional conservatives are more pragmatic.
- Both see private property ownership as a key element leading to social responsibility and order.
- Both movements are nationalist in outlook and have been determined to pursue British national interests.

Now test yourself

3 Look at the policies and ideas below. In each case, tick the appropriate column to indicate whether they belong to the New Right conservative tradition or to traditional conservatism.

Ideas/policies	New Right	Traditional
1 A belief in the organic society		
2 Support for traditional institutions		
3 Curbing trade union power		
4 A pragmatic approach to policy making		
5 Non-interference by government in economic management		

Answers on p. 104

Conservatism under David Cameron

Revised

How does conservatism under David Cameron compare with other traditions? The Conservative Party under Cameron can be seen as a combination of neoliberalism, traditional conservatism and liberalism. It has also been influenced by the need to retain a consensus between the Conservative Party and its Liberal Democrat partners in coalition. Its main features are summarised below.

Traditional conservative elements

- Cameron and his supporters tend to adopt a pragmatic approach to politics.
- They are committed to traditional institutions and values.
- They are committed to protecting the rights and interests of property owners.
- They believe that the wealthy do have a responsibility to help to improve the conditions of the disadvantaged.

New Right elements

- The party is still committed to free markets and maximising economic competition.
- Cameron and his supporters seek to keep direct taxes as low as possible.
- They are committed to financial responsibility and preventing the state overspending and interfering in economic activity.
- They hope to promote more competition and private sector involvement in the provision of services to the welfare state.
- They seek to target welfare benefits on those in most need and to attack benefits which are seen as a disincentive to work.

Liberal elements

- They accept diversity in society and promote tolerance of different groups and cultures.
- They are seeking to strengthen the protection of individual rights and liberties.
- They accept the need to reduce inequality in society.
- The 'Big Society' idea encourages voluntary community action and local democracy.
- There is cautious interest in constitutional reforms.
- The Conservative Party is placing more emphasis on environmental protection than ever before.

Conservative Party factions and tendencies

Revised

The Conservative Party is not totally united. There are now three factions or tendencies. They are shown in the Table 2.3.

> **Factionalism** is a tendency for political parties to split into groups who hold views that are different from the mainstream ideas and policies of the party.

Table 2.3 Conservative Party factions

Faction	Ideals	Leading members
Conservative Way Forward	Embraces the policies of Margaret Thatcher from the 1980s, including neoliberalism and neoconservatism.	Christopher Chope MP Lord Tebbitt Don Porter
Tory Reform Group	They see themselves as traditional 'One Nation' conservatives. They are liberal in their philosophy, supporting social justice, individual liberty and moderate law and order policies.	Kenneth Clarke MP Damian Green MP Alistair Burt MP
Cameronian conservatives	Supporters of David Cameron's philosophy, a combination of neoliberalism, orthodox liberalism, welfare reform and the Big Society.	David Cameron MP George Osborne MP Andrew Lansley MP

Traditions of the Labour Party — Revised

The Labour Party was founded at the start of the twentieth century.
Though it tended towards socialism, it was never a purely 'socialist' party.
The beliefs of the traditional Labour Party are summarised in Table 2.4.

> **Socialism** is a doctrine that emerged in the eighteenth century, but which came to fruition in the twentieth. It includes such ideas as collectivism, equality, the collective ownership of the means of production and state economic planning.

Typical mistake

Traditionally, the Labour Party was never a truly socialist party and it is a mistake to describe it as such. It was, however, based on a milder form of socialism known as 'democratic socialism' or 'social democracy'.

Table 2.4 Labour Party traditions

Ideas and principles	Examples of ideas and principles reflected in practical policies
Equality. People are essentially of equal worth and there should be no unjustified privileges or inequality in society. People are also entitled to equal rights.	• Artificial privileges should be removed or reduced. • Taxation and welfare benefits should be used to reduce differences in real incomes. • Wealth should not give anyone unjustified access to power.
Collectivism and universalism. They believe that most people prefer to achieve their goals collectively, rather than individually. Man is seen as a social animal or balances his own interests against those of the wider community. Furthermore, the collective provision of welfare should apply to all equally and universally.	• There should be a welfare state whereby such goods as health care, education, subsidised housing, social insurance, pensions and social care are paid for out of general taxation and all should be equally entitled to their benefits. • Local government services are a vital aspect of collectivism. • Workers are best protected by unions rather than through laws protecting individuals.
Control of capitalism. Capitalism can be tolerated but only if the exploitation of workers and consumers can be controlled, and if private enterprise serves the interests of the whole community.	• Key industries, including those providing infrastructure, energy and utilities, plus any natural monopolies, should be brought under public ownership and state control (nationalisation). • Strong trade unions to defend the interests of workers. • Control over monopoly power.

(Continued)

Table 2.4 Labour Party traditions (*continued*)

Ideas and principles	Examples of ideas and principles reflected in practical policies
Social justice. A belief and aspiration that all in society should have equal opportunities, should have access to a decent standard of living and should be able to improve their circumstance through their own merit.	• Provide education and other welfare benefits to widen personal opportunity. • The welfare state to guarantee living standards. • Strong laws to guarantee equal rights and to outlaw discrimination.
Class and society. Labour Party tradition argues that there is a fundamental division in society between classes, mainly the middle and working classes. The differences between classes need to be reconciled.	• The standard of living of the working class to be subsidised through progressive taxation and welfare provisions. • Strong trade unions represent the interests of the working class. • Firm economic management to control unemployment. • Controls over capitalism to reduce its exploitation of the working class. • Nationalisation to give the working class a greater stake in the economy.

What was New Labour?

Revised

The term 'New Labour' refers to the change that took place in the party from the middle of the 1990s under the leadership of John Smith and Tony Blair. It was a much more moderate, less left-wing party than traditional Labour. The main beliefs of New Labour, also known as the 'Third Way', are shown in Table 2.5.

Examiner's tip

Examiners are always interested in how the ideas and policies of the parties have changed over time. Make sure you are very familiar with these developments.

Table 2.5 New Labour and the 'Third Way'

Ideas and principles	Examples of ideas and principles reflected in practical policies
Individualism. The old collectivist ideas of Labour were replaced by a greater emphasis on individualism — the ability of the individual to realise his or her own goals and aspirations.	• Lower personal taxation, introduced by the Conservatives, to be retained to encourage work and enterprise. • Home ownership to be encouraged and supported. • Small businesses to be encouraged and supported. • A stress on education, including the expansion of higher education, to maximise the ability of individuals to widen their opportunities and to be socially mobile, in order to improve their living standards and status.
The free market. New Labour accepted that free market capitalism was the best form of wealth creator. The state should take control of enterprises only when they cannot be made to act in the public interest.	• No return to nationalisation of industries and some further privatisation to take place when justified. • Reduced corporate taxes to encourage enterprise, innovation and investment. • Private sector enterprises to be able to compete with public sector organisations in such areas as school and hospital building, local government services, prisons and road maintenance. • Weak trade unions to ensure free labour markets.
Welfare state. New Labour fully supported the welfare state and increased state spending in that area. However, welfare benefits were to be used as an incentive, rather than a disincentive to work and self-reliance. Welfare to be targeted to those in most need rather than simply universal.	• Increased spending on health and education. • Welfare benefits to be reformed and targeted on those in most need and withheld from those who do not seek work. • Improved efficiency by allowing the private sector to compete to provide services for the welfare state.

(Continued)

Table 2.5 New Labour and the 'Third Way' (continued)

Ideas and principles	Examples of ideas and principles reflected in practical policies
Social justice. New Labour shared many of the beliefs and ideas of traditional Labour.	• Provide education and other welfare benefits to widen personal opportunity. Special stress on higher education and pre-school education. • The welfare state to guarantee living standards. • Strong laws to guarantee equal rights and to outlaw discrimination. • The minimum wage to eliminate unacceptably low wages. • A general attack on child poverty through the welfare and education systems. • The tax credit system to guarantee minimum standards of living.
Communitarianism. New Labour replaced the old Labour belief in the class system with an idea known as communitarianism. This is a belief that, in a world of free market capitalism and individualism, all still have a responsibility to care for the community collectively.	• A caring attitude to the environment, with strong green policies. • An emphasis on schools, local welfare services and strong social services. • State support for local voluntary associations.
Ethical foreign policy. A belief that the UK has a responsibility for poorer parts of the world and that caring for the developing world is in the UK's self-interest.	• Increasing foreign aid. • Campaigning to cancel Third World debt. • Campaigning for more free market policies in world trade. • Intervening abroad where democracy and human rights are threatened.

Comparing New Labour and traditional Labour — Revised

How do New Labour and traditional Labour differ?

Differences

The main distinctions can be summarised as follows:

● New Labour stresses individualism, whereas old Labour stresses collectivism.

● Old Labour sought to modify and regulate capitalism, creating a mixed economy of both public and private sectors. New Labour accepts free market capitalism and encourages it.

● Old Labour saw the state as a key means by which society can be improved. New Labour sees the role of the state as merely enabling individuals to prosper.

● Old Labour saw society in terms of class conflict, while New Labour thinks class is insignificant and that individual interests are more important than class interests.

● Old Labour sought to promote economic and social equality, whereas New Labour sees inequality as natural and can be tolerable as long as there is equality of opportunity and opportunities are enhanced.

Similarities

The main similarities can be summarised as follows:

● Both strands believe in fundamental social justice — that excessive inequality in society is unacceptable.

● They believe that the welfare state is a key element in creating and maintaining social justice.

● They believe that there should be widespread equality of opportunity.

Exam practice answers and quick quizzes at **www.therevisionbutton.co.uk/myrevisionnotes**

- They believe there should be equal rights and no artificial discrimination against any sections of society.
- They believe that in a capitalist society, private enterprises need to be regulated to ensure they do not act against the public interest.

Now test yourself

4 Look at the policies and ideas below. In each case, tick the appropriate column to indicate whether they are closer to New Labour or traditional Labour.

Policy or idea	New Labour	Traditional Labour
1 A belief in strong trade unions		
2 Low corporate taxation		
3 Regulation of free market capitalism		
4 Very progressive tax to redistribute income		
5 Stress on individualism rather than collectivism		

Answers on p. 104

Modern Labour

Revised

After the party's 2010 election defeat, Ed Miliband became its new leader. Developments under Miliband are listed below:

- Labour will continue to emphasise education as the main driver of social justice and social mobility.
- There are likely to be more state interventions in certain key sectors of the economy. This may involve new company tax policies and public investment in industry: in other words, more state intervention than under New Labour. The industries concerned might include green technology, information technology, biomedical research and technology, and electronics.
- There is generally to be greater stress on environmental protection.
- The party now favours more active state intervention to promote economic growth.

Labour Party factions and tendencies

Revised

Like the Conservatives, Labour contains different tendencies. These are shown below:

- **New Labour traditionalists** — those who support the principles of the 'Third Way' developed in the 1990s. Harriet Harman MP, David Miliband MP and Ed Balls MP are important examples.
- **The left** — those who still support many traditional Labour policies, including radical redistribution of income, the restoration of trade union power and the return of some major industries to state control.
- **The right**— this group, sometimes referred to as 'Blue Labour', support a number of Conservative Party policies including the Big

Examiner's tip

Examiners expect you to know differences in policy both *within* and *between* parties.

Society, opposition to high levels of immigration and more local control over health and education. Leading figures are Maurice (Lord) Stearman and Dr Marc Stears.

What is traditional liberalism?

Revised

The ideology of liberalism dates back to the late eighteenth century. It has been a central feature of political life in the UK ever since. All three main parties accept most of its basic ideas. These are:

- the vital importance of individual liberties and rights
- equal rights for individuals and groups
- the destruction of artificial privileges
- tolerance of differing beliefs, movements and cultures
- constitutionalism — a belief that there need to be strict legal rules to determine the operation of government and politics
- limited government to prevent the concentration of power in the state
- the maximisation of democracy and the dispersal of power as widely as possible

Liberalism is a political doctrine originating in the eighteenth century. It expresses such ideas as individual liberty, equal rights, constitutionalism, tolerance and social justice.

The ideas of the Liberal Democrat Party

Revised

The Liberal Democrat Party was formed in 1988 through the amalgamation of the minor Liberal Party and the relatively new Social Democrat Party. The main beliefs of the party are summarised in Table 2.6.

Typical mistake

It is dangerous to assume that each party's beliefs correspond exactly to the three ideologies of liberalism, conservatism and socialism. In fact, their policies and beliefs correspond only loosely to the basic ideologies.

Table 2.6 Liberal Democrat beliefs

Ideas and principles	Examples of ideas and principles reflected in practical policies
Liberalism	• Strong laws to protect rights and liberties. • Tolerance enshrined in anti-discrimination laws. • Equal rights legislation.
Constitutionalism	• Support for the introduction of a codified, entrenched constitution controlling governmental power and dispersing power. • Constitutional reform proposals to modernise, liberalise, democratise and decentralise government and politics.
Social justice	• Taxation policies to redistribute real income from rich to poor. Higher taxes for the very rich. • Policies in education and employment to widen opportunity and increase social mobility.
Liberal law and order position	• Policies that recognise that crime is largely caused by poor social conditions. • Sentencing to take account of the social causes of crime and directed at rehabilitation rather than merely punishment.
Welfarism	• Strong support for the welfare state. • Welfare benefits to reduce poverty, support the disadvantaged and promote the value of work. • Education seen as the key driver for social justice.

(Continued)

Table 2.6 Liberal Democrat beliefs (*continued*)

Ideas and principles	Examples of ideas and principles reflected in practical policies
European Union	• The European Union is a positive force and should be supported and integration encouraged. • The UK should become more integrated in the European Union. • The UK should adopt the euro as soon as feasible.
Environmentalism	• Very ambitious plans for control over climate change. • Policies to transfer the UK to renewable energy sources as soon as possible.
Localism	• Local taxation to be reformed to make it 'fairer'. • Strengthening local government in comparison to central government. • Improving local democracy.

Check your understanding

Tested ☐

1 What is a political party?
2 Identify three functions of political parties.
3 Identify two current Conservative policies.
4 Identify two current Labour policies.
5 Identify two current Liberal Democrat policies.
6 Identify two policies that enjoy a wide consensus of support.
7 Identify two policies that are subject to adversary politics.

Answers on p. 104

Exam practice

Part (a) questions

1 Outline two of the main features of political parties. [5]
2 Outline two policies on which the coalition government partners disagree. [5]
3 Outline two ideas associated with traditional conservatism. [5]
4 Outline two ideas associated with liberalism. [5]

Part (b) questions

5 Explain the meaning of the term 'Thatcherism'. [10]
6 Explain what is meant by the term 'New Labour'. [10]
7 Explain how the Liberal Democrat Party is a 'liberal' party. [10]
8 Explain three ways in which current Conservative policies differ from Thatcherism. [10]

Part (c) questions

9 Distinguish between traditional Labour ideas and the current Labour Party's ideas. [25]
10 To what extent did Thatcherism differ from traditional conservatism? [25]
11 How far are all three main parties now 'liberal' parties? [25]
12 To what extent is current British politics consensual in nature? [25]

Answers and quick quiz 2 online

Online ☐

Examiner's summary

✔ Parties have special features that need to be known.

✔ Parties have many functions. The most important of these functions are vital to the workings of a modern liberal democracy.

✔ The left/right split in politics is a familiar idea. It gives a rough guide concerning the positioning of policies and ideas in the political spectrum.

✔ Conservatism is one of three key political traditions in the UK. It can be divided into traditional conservatism, the New Right and contemporary conservatism.

✔ The second political tradition is a mild form of socialism represented by the Labour Party. Labour is generally divided into 'old' or traditional Labour and 'New Labour'.

✔ Liberalism is the third political tradition. All mainstream politicians in the UK are more or less liberal. However, the Liberal Democrats are the most liberal-minded of them all.

✔ All three parties have policies and ideas that are in common with their traditions or are in conflict with them.

✔ All parties have internal factions and tendencies. Knowledge of these helps to understand their behaviour and development.

Exam practice answers and quick quizzes at **www.therevisionbutton.co.uk/myrevisionnotes**

3 Elections

The main elements of this section of the specification are these. First, students need to develop an understanding of the various roles that elections play in a democracy. This includes knowledge and understanding of how they operate and why they differ from referendums. Secondly, it is necessary to develop an understanding of, and an ability to evaluate, the extent to which elections enhance democracy or are undemocratic. Thirdly, students need to be able to explain how all systems operating in the UK operate and the nature of their impact. Finally, it is necessary to understand and assess the arguments for and against electoral reform in the UK.

Elections and democracy

What are the roles of elections? Revised

Elections are the main way in which most people participate in politics; for many they are the *only* type of political activity. Elections are mainly held to elect representatives, but serve a number of other functions. These are described below:

- Elections are a way in which votes are converted into representation.
- Elections of a single person, such as a mayor, have the function of granting democratic legitimacy to a single office-holder.
- Other elections return representatives to representative assemblies. These might be a local council, a regional parliament or assembly, the UK Parliament in Westminster, or the European Parliament.
- When electing a government, they grant a mandate to that government, giving it the authority to implement its electoral commitments (manifesto).
- They give the electorate the opportunity to call existing governments and representatives to account.
- They enable the electorate to choose between alternative political programmes and prospective leaders.
- They give opportunities for citizens to participate actively in the political process, and so they secure their consent.
- They are a means by which the electorate can be informed and educated about political issues.

> An **election** is a device by which popular votes can be converted into seats awarded to representatives or parties, or used to elect single office-holders or political leaders.

> A **mandate** is the authority granted to a candidate or party to implement its manifesto commitments. The mandate is normally granted by election.

How do elections enhance democracy?

Here the question is the extent to which elections enhance modern democracy, and the extent to which they have features that may not be democratic. Table 3.1 shows these two aspects of elections.

Table 3.1 Elections and democracy

Positive features	Negative features
• They are a means of granting legitimacy. • They give a clear mandate to governments. • They are a means of calling government and representatives to account. • They offer democratic choices to the people. • They provide opportunities for participation in politics. • They educate and inform the people on political issues.	• They limit choice because parties produce specific manifestos but people are interested in individual issues. • In the case of the UK especially, elections may not be fair and proportional. • Elections often exclude small parties. • The mandate that elections grant to governments may give them excessive power. • Because of their expense, elections may help those with most financial resources.

Now test yourself

1   Make a list of **four** positive and **four** negative features of elections to the UK Parliament.

Answers on p. 105

Distinctions between elections and referendums

Table 3.2 demonstrates the key distinctions.

Table 3.2 Distinctions between elections and referendums

Elections	Referendums
• Deal with a wide range of issues.	• Are concerned with a single issue.
• Elect representatives.	• Do not elect anyone.
• Are held at regular intervals.	• May be held at any time.
• Give a complex range of answers.	• Give one simple 'yes' or 'no' answer.
• Concern political parties.	• Usually cut across party differences.

Elections in the UK

How does first-past-the-post operate?

First-past-the-post (FPTP) is the name commonly given to the electoral system used to elect members of the House of Commons in Westminster, and therefore, to elect the government. Its formal name is **simple plurality in single-member constituencies.** This is how it operates:

- The country is divided into 650 constituencies of roughly equal size.
- The number of constituencies is likely to fall by 10% before 2015 and the size to be adjusted to make them more exactly equal.
- Each constituency elects one Member of Parliament (MP).

- Voters choose from a list of candidates, nearly all of whom have been nominated by a political party.
- The candidate who receives most votes is elected.
- It is not necessary for the winning candidate to obtain more than half the votes cast (i.e. they win with a plurality, rather than an absolute majority).

Typical mistake

Candidates often confuse *plurality* with *majority*. Plurality means that a candidate has more votes than any other. It does not necessarily mean that he or she has an overall majority – i.e. over 50%. Majority means more than 50%, or more than all other candidates' votes added together.

Main characteristics and impacts of first-past-the-post

The first-past-the-post electoral system produces a number of interesting and remarkable outcomes. These are the main ones:

- The result, in terms of the distribution of seats between parties in the House of Commons, is not proportionate to overall support for each of the parties. For example:
  - Labour won the 2005 election (i.e. won over 50% of the seats) with only 35% of the popular vote.
  - The Conservatives won 36% of the total votes in 2010, but this converted to 47% of the seats.
  - The Liberal Democrats won 23% of the total votes in 2010, but only 9% of the seats.
- The system favours parties that have concentrated support, such as the Labour and Conservative parties. This is because parties with support that is spread out rarely finish top of the ballot in any constituency.
- Very small parties, such as the Greens, the BNP and UKIP, normally cannot win any seats (though the Greens won one in 2010). This keeps out both extreme, undemocratic parties, and small parties that represent minority views.
- It creates many 'safe' seats where the result is an inevitable win for one of the parties.
- Voters in safe seats have less influence on the outcome, so votes are of unequal value.
- Many votes for small parties are effectively 'wasted'.
- Because it favours the large parties, it tends to produce a clear winner with one party winning an overall majority of seats in the Commons.
- The winner therefore often has a clear mandate and can govern decisively.
- The result above is not guaranteed, however, as no party won such a majority in 2010.

Strong government refers to a government that can rely upon a strong majority of support in Parliament and so is able to carry through its own legislation and other proposals.

Stable government refers to a government that is likely to remain in office without serious crises. Such a government will probably not become divided or fall from power before its term of office is complete.

Examiner's tip

When you are discussing first-past-the-post, the examiners will certainly need to know why it discriminates against some parties. Make sure you can explain this clearly in an examination.

What other electoral systems are used in the UK?

Electoral systems used in the UK are listed in Table 3.3.

Table 3.3 Electoral systems in the UK

System	Where used
Additional member system (AMS)	Scottish Parliament Welsh Assembly Greater London Assembly
Single transferable vote (STV)	Northern Ireland Assembly Northern Ireland local government Scottish local government
Regional list	European Parliament
Supplementary vote (SV)	Elected mayors

Proportional representation is any electoral system, allied to a political system, that apportions seats in the legislature in close proportion to the popular vote cast for each party.

Typical mistake

Many exam candidates think that proportional representation is an electoral system. This is not true. PR describes any system that tends to produce proportional results.

Examiner's tip

You need to be up to date with your knowledge. For example, be able to illustrate answers with results from the most recent elections to the UK Parliament, devolved assemblies or the European Parliament, or from London elections. These demonstrate the impact of different electoral systems.

How other electoral systems work

How electoral systems other than first-past-the-post work is described in Table 3.4.

Typical mistake

The specification states that only knowledge of systems currently used in the UK is needed. So it is a mistake to describe any others. You only need know about a system not used in the UK, such as AV, if you are discussing the possibility of electoral reform in very general terms.

Examiner's tip

Examiners are looking for candidates who understand the basic workings of electoral systems in the UK. This does not mean that you need to give a very long drawn-out account, but a description of the system that demonstrates a secure knowledge of the fundamentals.

Table 3.4 How electoral systems work

System	Operation
Additional member system	• A proportion (about two-thirds) of the seats are elected by first-past-the-post (FPTP). • The rest of the seats are elected though a regional list system. • In the list system, voters choose between parties, not candidates. • Seats in the list section are awarded according the proportion of votes for each party, adjusted according to the extent to which parties are discriminated against under FPTP.
Single transferable vote	• Each constituency returns several representatives, usually six. • An electoral quota is calculated – the number of votes, divided by the number of seats plus 1, then 1 is added to the total. • Voters may vote for as many or as few candidates as they wish. They may vote for one candidate only or all the candidates. • Candidates who reach the quota on first choices are automatically elected. • Second and subsequent preferences of votes for candidates already elected are then added to the rest of the candidates. This continues until six candidates achieve the quota.
Regional list (the system in the UK is known as 'closed list')	• Each party presents a list of candidates in its chosen order of preference. • Voters have one vote which they cast for a party list, not an individual candidate. • Seats are awarded to each party broadly in proportion to the votes cast for that party.
Supplementary vote	• This is used to elect a single individual. • Each voter chooses a first and second preference. • If one candidate secures over 50% of the first preferences of voters, he or she is elected. • If not, all but the top two candidates are eliminated. • The second preferences cast for each of the top two candidates are then added and the winner is the candidate with more votes when first and second preferences are added together.

> **Examiner's tip**
>
> It is particularly important to demonstrate knowledge of how various electoral systems impact upon the political system. This means three things: first, the impact upon voters and voting behaviour; secondly, the impact upon the party system (how many parties are likely to win representation?); and thirdly, the impact on government formation (does it tend to produce minority party systems, coalitions or single-party government?).

Features and impacts of other electoral systems   Revised

Table 3.5 overleaf indicates the main features and impacts of electoral systems other than first-past-the-post used in the UK.

> **Majoritarian representation** is any system which guarantees that a government or a single individual is elected by an overall majority of voters. This applies to the SV and AV systems.
>
> A **party system** is a characteristic of a political system which describes how many parties win significant representation. Systems may be dominant party, two party, three party or multi-party.

Table 3.5 Features and impacts of electoral systems

Electoral system	Features	Impacts
Additional member system	• Voters have two choices. • It helps small parties. • The outcome is very proportional. • It retains the constituency system.	• In Scotland it produced a four-party system. There were two-party coalitions until 2011 when, surprisingly, it produced an absolute majority for the Scottish Nationalist Party. • In Wales there is also a four-party system. It has always produced two-party coalition government. • In the Greater London Assembly, six parties have won seats.
Single transferable vote	• Voters have a very wide choice. • The outcome is very proportional. • Voters may discriminate between candidates of the same party. • It retains constituencies but most people have a representative who represents their own favoured party.	• In the Northern Ireland Assembly, five different parties gain significant numbers of seats. • This gives rise to a power-sharing government (all large parties represented in government). • In local government it produces multi-party representation.
Regional list	• Voters choose parties, not candidates. • Every vote is of exactly equal value. • The outcome is highly proportional.	• Six different parties gained seats in the European Parliament.
Supplementary vote	• Each voter has two choices. • The winner is guaranteed an overall majority.	• It is a successful way of electing single individuals with a clear mandate.

Now test yourself

Tested ☐

2 Copy this table and fill in the missing details to show which electoral systems operate where, and their features and impacts.

Political system	Electoral system	Features, party system and typical type of government
Scottish Parliament	_____	• Some candidates stand in constituencies; others are on regional party lists. • _____ • _____ • _____
_____	Single transferable vote	• _____ • _____ • _____
_____	Supplementary vote	• _____ • _____
European Parliament	_____	• Produces a very proportional result. • Voters choose parties, not individual candidates.

Answers on p. 105

Debating electoral systems

Arguments for and against electoral reform
Revised

First it is necessary to evaluate first-past-the-post separately.

Arguments for retaining first-past-the-post

- It has existed for a long time and is widely accepted.
- It is easy to understand.
- It retains a strong link between an MP and his or her constituency.
- It tends to produce single-party, decisive government with a clear House of Commons majority (though the 2010 result weakens this argument).

Arguments for abandoning first-past-the-post

- It is an unfair system that awards seats disproportionately between the parties.
- It produces large numbers of wasted votes — those in safe seats or for 'no-hope' parties.
- It means that votes are effectively not of equal value. Those in close, marginal seats are worth more than those in 'safe' seats where one party is certain to win.
- It discriminates significantly against small parties.
- The 2010 election result — a hung parliament with no overall majority — removes the main remaining reason for retaining first-past-the-post: that it produces a clear winner.
- Even when it does produce a government with a clear majority, it can be argued that it gives too much power to a party that does not win a majority of the votes.
- Most MPs are elected on less than 50% of the vote and governing parties are always elected with a minority of the popular vote. This leads to doubts about democratic legitimacy.
- Turnouts are low in historical terms (60–65% recently compared to past levels of 75%), suggesting the system is losing support.
- It is out of step with the rest of Europe. Nowhere else in Europe uses first-past-the-post.

Should the UK adopt proportional representation?
Revised

Table 3.6 shows the arguments for and against proportional representation — that is, any one of a number of systems including AMS, STV and the regional list system.

> **Electoral reform** is any process which involves changing the electoral system and thus effecting changes in the political system.

Table 3.6 Arguments for and against introducing proportional representation for main UK elections

For introduction	Against introduction
• It is fairer, making votes more equal and eliminating wasted votes. Turnout might therefore increase.	• The 'No' vote on the introduction of AV suggests there is little appetite for electoral reform in the UK.
• It would produce a proportional parliament and possibly restore confidence in the political process.	• Other systems may be more difficult for the electorate to understand and accept.
• It would help small parties, some of which represent minorities in society.	• It might give too many opportunities for small extremist parties to gain a foothold in politics.
• Preventing a single party from winning overall control would reduce the possibilities of an 'elective dictatorship'.	• If no party can win an overall majority in the UK Parliament, it may make for less decisive, weak and inefficient government.
• A multi-party system might usher in an era of more consensus politics.	• Some systems would weaken or destroy the MP–constituency link.
• It would bring the UK into line with the rest of Europe.	

Now test yourself

Tested ☐

3 Look at the following characteristics of various electoral systems. In each case, write in the name of an electoral system with that particular feature.

Feature	Electoral system
Voters choose a party rather than a candidate	
Voters are given the widest choice of candidates	
Produces the most proportional result	
Preserves the strongest MP–constituency link	
Is often used to elect a single office-holder	
Voters can vote both for a candidate and for a party	

Answers on p. 105

Check your understanding

Tested ☐

1 Describe first-past-the-post.
2 Describe the single transferable vote (STV) system.
3 Describe the additional member system (AMS).
4 Describe the regional list system.
5 Describe the supplementary vote (SV) system.
6 Describe three impacts of first-past-the-post.
7 Define 'proportional representation'.

Answers on p. 105

Exam practice

Part (a) questions

1 Explain two functions of elections.   [5]
2 Distinguish between an election and a referendum.   [5]
3 What is an electoral mandate?   [5]
4 What is an election manifesto?   [5]

Part (b) questions

5 Why has first-past-the-post been criticised as an electoral system?   [10]
6 What is the relationship between proportional representation and the party system?   [10]
7 Explain the main impacts of any two electoral systems other than first-past-the-post.   [10]
8 Why is proportional representation used for elections to the Scottish Parliament and Welsh Assembly? [10]

Part (c) questions

9   Assess the arguments for the introduction of proportional representation for UK general elections. [25]
10 To what extent do UK general elections enhance or damage democracy?   [25]
11 Assess the arguments for retaining the first-past-the-post electoral system.   [25]
12 Why has the first-past-the-post electoral system been criticised?   [25]

Answers and quick quiz 3 online

Online

Examiner's summary

- ✔ Elections have a number of functions above and beyond simply returning representatives to office.

- ✔ While it might be thought that elections are democratic in nature, in fact they can be seen both to enhance and to hinder democracy. Furthermore, some electoral systems are more democratic than others.

- ✔ The main British system is called first-past-the-post. This system is controversial and has both supporters and opponents. It has long been associated with the UK's two-party system and a strong executive.

- ✔ Other electoral systems are used in British regional and local elections, and elections to the European Parliament.

These are proportional systems and tend to produce a variety of party systems.

- ✔ There are strong connections between electoral systems and party systems, including typical forms of government — single party majority, minority and coalitions, for example.

- ✔ Although the 2011 referendum on AV resulted in a 'No' vote, the issue of electoral reform remains significant.

- ✔ The arguments for and against retaining first-past-the-post are quite evenly balanced.

- ✔ Similarly, there are balanced arguments for and against the introduction of proportional representation.

4 Pressure groups

Pressure groups have become increasingly important in modern British politics. As the influence and popularity of political parties has declined, so the number and membership of pressure groups has risen. They are key vehicles of representation, protect minority interests, help to control government power and help to disperse power more widely.

Nature of pressure groups

A definition of a pressure group should include the following facts:

- It is an association of people who share certain political goals.
- Pressure groups seek either to defend or further the interests of a particular section of society, or to promote a particular cause or issue.
- Despite having political goals, pressure groups do not seek governmental power, but merely to influence the political system.
- Pressure groups seek to mobilise as wide a level of support as possible to further their goals.

> **Pressure groups** are political associations that are dedicated to defending and promoting the interests of a section of the community, or that wish to pursue a particular cause in order to influence government at any level.

How are pressure groups normally classified? — Revised

Pressure groups are usually classified in two different ways according to whether they are:

- sectional or promotional groups
- insider or outsider groups

> **Sectional/promotional** groups are a way of classifying pressure groups into either sectional groups that represent a section of society, or promotional groups that pursue a cause or an issue.
>
> **Insider/outsider** groups are a way of classifying pressure groups into those that have influence inside governing circles and those that have to influence decision-makers from outside governing circles.

Typical mistake

It is wrong to assume that all pressure groups fall neatly into one or other of the categories 'sectional' and 'promotional'. Some groups are both. They believe that, by defending the interests of a specific group, they are also serving the interests of the whole society.

Sectional groups

These are pressure groups that represent a section of society. They are interested only in the interests of that group and have narrow goals.

Exam practice answers and quick quizzes at **www.therevisionbutton.co.uk/myrevisionnotes**

Examples: Confederation of British Industry (CBI), National Union of Students (NUS), British Bankers' Association (BBA), Royal College of Nurses (RCN), Age UK.

Promotional groups

These groups are concerned with a cause or an issue. They are open to all members of the community and are altruistic in that they believe that their cause or issue will benefit the community.

Examples: Friends of the Earth (FoE), Unlock Democracy, Action on Smoking and Health (ASH), Liberty, Council for the Protection of Rural England (CPRE).

Insider groups

Insider pressure groups are those that have special connections with government and Parliament. They have direct access to decision-makers and are involved with the development of policy. They have the following characteristics and methods:

- They are regularly consulted by ministers, civil servants and policy advisers.
- They are often also consulted by parliamentary committees.
- They sometimes have representatives sitting on policy and advisory committees.
- Those concerned with Europe have direct access to the European Commission and European Parliament.
- Regional groups have access to devolved administrations.
- Local pressure groups have access to local authorities.

Examples: National Union of Farmers (NFU), Royal Society for the Protection of Animals (RSPCA), Automobile Association (AA), National Society for the Prevention of Cruelty to Children (NSPCC).

Outsider groups

Outsider pressure groups do not have direct access to government or Parliament or decision-makers in general. This may be because they choose not to be an insider to maintain their independence or because decision-makers do not wish to be associated with them. Instead they tend to operate by mobilising public support and putting pressure on decision-makers by demonstrating how much support they have. They have the following characteristics and methods:

- They seek to mobilise public support.
- They often use **direct action** such as street demonstrations, publicity stunts or acts of civil disobedience.
- They seek to use media campaigns.
- They increasingly use the internet and social networks to build up support.
- They also use petitions, often online.

Examples: Greenpeace, Plane Stupid, Animal Liberation Front, Countryside Alliance, Exit (voluntary euthanasia).

Functional representation refers to the idea that various groups represent sections of society that have particular functions — particularly occupational, social, economic and producer groups.

Now test yourself

1 (a) Consider the pressure groups listed below. In each case, indicate whether they are likely to be a sectional or a promotional group by ticking the appropriate column.

Group	Sectional	Promotional
National Union of Mineworkers		
Amnesty International		
National Trust		
Taxpayers' Alliance		
Campaign for Real Ale		

(b) Now state whether the following groups are insiders or outsiders.

Group	Insider	Outsider
Greenpeace		
National Farmers' Union		
RSPCA		
Countryside Alliance		

Answers on p. 106

How do pressure groups and parties differ?

Revised

These are the main distinctions between pressure groups and political parties:

- Parties actively seek to gain governmental power or a share of power; pressure groups do not seek power.
- Parties must develop policies across the full range of government business; pressure groups have narrow goals, normally concentrating on one issue or the narrow interests of one group.
- Parties have to make themselves accountable for their policies; pressure groups do not.
- Parties normally have a formal organisation; pressure groups may be formally organised, but are often very loose organisations.

However, the distinction between parties and pressure groups can be unclear, for the following reasons:

- Pressure groups sometimes put up candidates for election in order to publicise their goals or issue. However, this does not mean they seek power, merely influence.
- Some pressure groups develop a wide range of policies like parties. Trade unions and the CBI are examples.
- Sometimes pressure groups transform themselves into parties and there may be confusion over such transitional groups — the Green Party began as a pressure group, as did UKIP.
- Some pressure groups are very closely associated with parties. This used to be the case with trade unions and Labour (and still is to some extent), and it is true of groups like the Countryside Alliance which has strong links with the Conservatives.

Examiner's tip

In questions that ask for distinctions between parties and pressure groups, the examiners expect candidates to indicate that the distinctions are not always clear.

Exam practice answers and quick quizzes at **www.therevisionbutton.co.uk/myrevisionnotes**

What is pluralism?

Pluralism is both a concept and a description of either a society or a political system. It has these meanings:

- It means any situation where a variety of ideas and groups can flourish together.
- It can mean that power within a political system is widely dispersed and not concentrated in a few hands.
- In society as a whole it means that a variety of beliefs, cultures, lifestyles and ethnic groups exist together and are broadly tolerated.
- A pluralist democracy is one which recognises the right of different groups to have influence and to receive equal treatment.

> **Pluralism** is a description of a society or a political system which suggests that there are many groups, beliefs, cultures and lifestyles that flourish together and are recognised and tolerated.

What is elitism?

In many ways, elitism is the opposite of pluralism. It is mostly used as a description of the distribution of power within a political system or society. In detail:

- It generally means that there is a concentration of political, social or economic power within a few hands.
- It can describe a political system within which a small number of individuals or bodies hold most of the available power.
- It therefore implies that most groups in society are denied power or influence.

> **Elitism** is a description of a society or a political system which suggests that power – political, social and economic – resides in the hands of a small number of people, often known as elites.

Typical mistake

It is wrong to assume that all pressure groups fall neatly into one or other of the categories 'sectional' and 'promotional'. Some groups are both. They believe that, by defending the interests of a specific group, they are also serving the interests of the whole society.

Pluralism, elitism and pressure groups

What is the relationship between pluralism, elitism and pressure groups?

Pressure groups enhance pluralism in these senses:

- They disperse power and influence very widely (especially mass membership groups).
- They ensure that many groups are able to exert political influence.
- They help to protect the interests of groups in society (sectional groups).
- They balance the power of centralised government.

Pressure groups can be associated with elitism in these senses:

- Some powerful, wealthy, influential pressure groups may concentrate power in few hands (for example, large producer groups).
- Influential insider groups may serve to concentrate more power in government hands.
- Some pressure groups may be led by unaccountable elites.
- Some groups may hold a disproportionate amount of power.

Pressure group power

Why are pressure groups becoming more important?

Revised

It is generally accepted that pressure group activity is becoming more extensive and more significant. The list below includes the main reasons for this:

- Membership of, and identification with, political parties is declining. Pressure group activity replaces this to some extent.
- Arguably the electorate is now better informed and is therefore more able to become involved in political issues.
- The internet and new social media have made it more practicable to mount campaigns and initiate new associations.
- Both the number of pressure groups and their membership have greatly increased. Some groups have millions of members and supporters.
- Society has become more pluralistic and fragmented into groups which have special interests. This is reflected in the proliferation of interest groups.
- Arguably the political system is now more accessible to group activity, there are more points of access and politicians are more sensitive to public opinion.
- Growing affluence means that the population have more interests and thus make more demands on the political system.

> **Examiner's tip**
>
> Examiners are especially looking for responses that show how the role and importance of pressure groups is *changing* over time: that is, how and why their methods are changing and how and why they are becoming more important.

What are the main methods used by pressure groups?

Revised

Pressure groups use a variety of methods, depending on their circumstances and status and the nature of the issue they are pursuing. Table 4.1 details the main methods used, offers some reasons why they are used and gives examples of pressure groups that typically use them.

Table 4.1 Pressure group methods

Method	Why used	Examples
Lobbying ministers	Insiders feel they can influence decisions and policy.	Confederation of British Industry
Sitting on advisory and policy committees in government	They can supply specialist information and advice.	British Medical Association
Lobbying European Union institutions	Most of their concerns are under the jurisdiction of the EU.	National Farmers' Union
Lobbying local councillors and officers	Concerns are local in nature.	Local conservation groups
Organising mass public demonstrations	They have widespread support but are outsiders.	Stop the [Iraq] War campaign
Media campaigns	Celebrities are involved and the issue captures the public imagination.	Justice for Ghurkhas campaign
Civil disobedience	Outsiders need to attract publicity.	Greenpeace
Internet campaigns	Probably issues that appeal mostly to the young.	Friends of the Earth
Action through the law courts	The rights of members are threatened.	Trade unions

Exam practice answers and quick quizzes at **www.therevisionbutton.co.uk/myrevisionnotes**

Tested

Now test yourself

2 For each of the following methods used by pressure groups, give two examples of pressure groups that are most likely to use them.

   (a) Civil disobedience

   (b) Sitting on policy advisory committees

   (c) Lobbying the European Union

   (d) Organising public demonstrations

Answers on p. 106

Why are some pressure groups more successful?

Revised

Table 4.2 indicates the main factors in the success of some pressure groups. The table also gives some examples and indicates the nature of the success that the groups enjoyed.

Examiner's tip

When answering questions about the 'success' of pressure groups, it is important to say what 'success' means — promoting friendly legislation, preventing unfriendly legislation, promoting legislative amendments, or merely getting an issue on to the political agenda.

Table 4.2 Pressure group success

Factor	Pressure group	Evidence of success
Resources — financial and organisational, giving a group the ability and people to mount a major campaign	The **Countryside Alliance** organised mass demonstrations in London.	Anti-fox hunting legislation was successfully watered down in 2004.
Insider status — being established in government circles and well trusted	**Action on Smoking and Health**	A series of pieces of legislation were introduced to deter and reduce smoking.
Tactics — groups may find a good formula for influencing government and/or mobilising public support	The **Save England's Forests** campaign used a variety of tactics, including a huge e-petition, celebrity campaigners, demonstrations and MP involvement.	Government plans to sell off large quantities of publicly owned forest in 2010 were cancelled.
Sharing the same agenda as the government — helps greatly when campaigning for change	The **Confederation of British Industry** welcomed a new business-friendly government in 2010.	It secured a commitment by government to reduce corporation tax on company profits by 14% over 4 years.
Lack of opposition	**Make Poverty History**, a campaign group of the 1990s and 2000s, experienced little opposition to its championing of developing countries.	Governments raised their commitments to foreign debt relief and increased overseas aid.
Favourable circumstances	**Action on Smoking and Health** was helped by reductions in cases of lung cancer following anti-smoking legislation.	Eventually ASH secured a ban on smoking in public places in 2006.
Celebrity involvement	The **Justice for Ghurkas** campaign led by actress Joanna Lumley demanded that retired Gurkhas (Nepalese troops serving in the British army) should have the right to settle in the UK.	The campaign was dramatically successful and the government was forced, in 2009, to reverse its policies denying Gurkhas the right to stay in the UK.
Strategic position	The **British Bankers' Association** (BBA) used its representation of powerful banks to campaign against banking reform. The government feared that large banks might move away from the UK if their operations were curbed.	Plans to limit banks' awards of excessive bonuses and high salaries were watered down considerably in 2011.

Summary: important examples of pressure groups

Table 4.3 identifies a number of important pressure groups together with some of the features and aspects of their importance.

Table 4.3 Key examples of important pressure groups

Group	Sectional or promotional?	Insider or outsider?	Disperse or concentrate power?	Typical methods
British Bankers' Association	Sectional	Insider	Concentrate	Lobbying ministers
Greenpeace	Promotional	Outsider	Disperse	Direct action, civil disobedience
Liberty	Promotional	Outsider	Disperse	Media campaigns
Countryside Alliance	Sectional	Outsider	Disperse	Media campaigns, public demonstrations, civil disobedience
Institute of Directors	Sectional	Insider	Concentrate	Lobbying, places on advisory committees, evidence to Parliament

Typical mistake

The most common mistake made by candidates is to fail to use examples of real pressure groups when analysing their features and activities.

Examiner's tip

Examiners are especially interested in the use of appropriate examples. This includes not only knowledge of pressure groups, but also knowledge of their activities and notable successes.

Pressure groups and democracy

Do pressure groups enhance or damage democracy?

On the whole, pressure groups are seen as an important element in modern democracy. However, there are senses in which they can be seen as undemocratic. The following two sections demonstrate this balance.

Ways in which pressure groups enhance democracy

- They often represent groups and causes that have been ignored by political parties.
- They help to disperse power more widely, preventing dangerous concentrations of power.
- They help to educate and inform the public about important issues.
- They may help the governing process by providing informed advice.
- They can act as a control mechanism against over-mighty government.
- They provide ways in which people can participate in politics, especially at a time when traditional forms of participation are declining.
- They provide an outlet for public grievances — a process known as 'tension release'.

Pluralist democracy is a political system within which many different groups are tolerated, allowed to flourish and able to influence decision making.

Ways in which pressure groups do not support democracy

- They may undermine the authority of elected officials and Parliament.
- They can be seen as representing the 'politics of self-interest' and may present the public with biased or even false information.
- If they are too powerful, they may create 'hyper-pluralism' which can hold up the process of government by being too obstructive.
- Pressure groups lack elective legitimacy and are not democratically accountable.
- Those that engage in civil disobedience threaten order in society and subvert democracy.
- Some wealthy or influential pressure groups may have more influence than can be justified.
- The leadership of some elitist groups may not reflect accurately the views of their membership.

Now test yourself

Tested ☐

3 Consider the following features of pressure groups and examples of their activity and decide whether they enhance or threaten democracy.

Activity	Enhance democracy	Threaten democracy
Campaigns of civil disobedience		
Mass membership		
Use of large amounts of finance		
Insider links with government		

Answers on p. 106

Check your understanding

Tested ☐

1 Identify three functions of pressure groups.
2 Identify three promotional pressure groups.
3 Identify three sectional pressure groups.
4 Identify two insider pressure groups.
5 Identify two outsider pressure groups.
6 Identify three types of direct action.
7 Give three reasons why some pressure groups are successful.
8 Give three reasons why some pressure groups are unsuccessful.

Answers on p. 106

Exam practice

Part (a) questions

1 Distinguish between sectional and promotional pressure groups. [5]
2 Distinguish between insider and outsider pressure groups. [5]
3 Distinguish between parties and pressure groups. [5]
4 Outline three methods used by insider pressure groups. [5]
5 Outline three methods used by outsider pressure groups. [5]
6 Define 'pluralism'. [5]
7 Define 'elitism'. [5]

Part (b) questions

8 Why can it be difficult to distinguish between parties and pressure groups? [10]
9 Why have pressure group methods changed in recent years? [10]
10 How and why do insider groups' methods differ from those used by outsider groups? [10]
11 How has the internet affected pressure group activity? [10]

Part (c) questions

12 To what extent do pressure groups enhance democracy? [25]
13 Why are some pressure groups more successful than others? [25]
14 How and why have pressure group methods changed in recent years? [25]
15 Explain the increased use of direct action by pressure groups. [25]
16 Do pressure groups mainly disperse or concentrate power? [25]

Answers and quick quiz 4 online

Online

Examiner's summary

✔ Pressure groups are a key element in a representative democracy. There are many different types of group, using different methods with varying degrees of success or failure.

✔ The classifications of pressure groups are important because they tell us a good deal about their features, goals and methods.

✔ Although it may seem clear that pressure groups enhance democracy, it is also true that some aspects of their behaviour, and some types of pressure group, can damage democracy and operate in an undemocratic way.

✔ The links between pressure groups, pluralism and elitism are most important. It is generally believed that pressure group activities help to disperse power. However, there are ways in which some of them can actually concentrate power in too few hands.

✔ Some pressure groups have a great deal more success than others. Both the nature of 'success' and the reasons why some groups are more successful than others should be understood.

✔ Pressure groups and parties should be compared in two senses: first, how they may be distinguished; and secondly, how and why pressure groups are becoming more important at the expense of parties.

✔ Pressure groups are subject constantly to change. Change can refer to their importance, their features and their methods.

5 The constitution

There are three main elements to the study of the constitution. The first concerns developing an understanding of the nature of constitutions and different types of constitution. Secondly, there is a need to understand the main issues and developments in the constitution, including codification and the changing nature and location of sovereignty. Thirdly, the true nature of the constitution should be understood and analysed, including evaluations of its strengths and weaknesses. Finally, the whole issue of reform must be understood, analysed and evaluated. This concerns a full knowledge of past, present and proposed constitutional reforms, including evaluations of their effectiveness and likely impacts.

Nature of the constitution

The role of a constitution
Revised ✓

Constitutions have the following functions:
- They establish the distribution of power within a political system.
- They establish the relationships between political institutions and individuals.
- They define and establish the limits of government power.
- They specify the rights of individual citizens and how they are to be protected.
- They define the nature of citizenship and how individuals may obtain citizenship.
- They establish the territory which comes under the jurisdiction of the government.
- They establish and describe the arrangements for amending the constitution.

A **constitution** is a set of rules that establish and describe the distribution of power within a state, the procedures of government, the limits to government power and rights of citizens as well as rules on citizenship and constitutional amendment. A constitution may be codified or uncodified, federal or unitary.

Constitutionalism is a principle that government operates within a set of constitutional rules and not in arbitrary fashion. The constitutional rules may be written or unwritten.

Typical mistake

Although the UK constitution is uncodified and cannot be found in a single document, this does not mean that it does not exist. It does, but is in many forms, some of them unwritten.

Codified and uncodified constitutions

A **codified constitution** has the following features:

- It is written in a single document.
- It is therefore said to have a single source.
- Constitutional laws are superior to other laws, a feature known as 'dualism'.
- Special arrangements exist to establish new constitutional laws, amend existing ones or repeal unwanted constitutional laws.
- Codified constitutions normally come into existence at one point in time, often after a national upheaval such as a revolution or the establishment of independence from a colonial master.
- Because the constitutional laws in a codified constitution are superior and safeguarded, they are said to be **entrenched**. That means they cannot be set aside or changed without special safeguarding arrangements.

An **uncodified constitution** has the following features:

- It is not written in a single document.
- It therefore has a number of different sources.
- Constitutional laws are not superior to other laws.
- The arrangements for changing the laws of the constitution are the same as those for passing other laws.
- Uncodified constitutions develop over time and are more flexible than codified constitutions.
- Because constitutional laws are not superior and can easily be changed, they are said to be **unentrenched**. They are not specially protected against change.

> **Codified/uncodified constitutions** refer to a classification of constitutions into two types. Codified constitutions are set down in a single constitution, have a single source, are entrenched and are superior to other laws. Uncodified constitutions have multiple sources, do not appear in a single document and are flexible.

Now test yourself

Tested

1 Look at each of the following characteristics and decide whether they apply to a codified or uncodified constitution.

Characteristic	Codified	Uncodified
It is not very flexible.		
It is a strong safeguard of rights.		
It can adapt to changing circumstances.		
It has a number of different sources.		
It can be easily interpreted by judges.		
It can be found in one single document.		
It is likely to be entrenched.		

Answers on p. 107

What is the nature of sovereignty?

Sovereignty is a key concept in relation to constitutions. Its meaning is this:

- It means ultimate power within a political system.
- It also means the ultimate source of political power.
- Legal sovereignty refers to the power to make laws. It is where power lies *theoretically*.
- Political sovereignty refers to the location of power in very general terms. It is where power lies *in reality*.
- When sovereignty is located in an institution or individual office-holder by a constitution, it cannot be overruled or changed without a constitutional amendment. However, political sovereignty is a more flexible concept.

Unitary and federal constitutions

The distinctions between these two types of constitution are these:

- In **unitary constitutions**, legal sovereignty lies in one place. In **federal constitutions**, legal sovereignty is divided between the centre and regional bodies.
- In unitary constitutions, any powers not assigned by law automatically fall to the body with legal sovereignty; in the case of the UK, this is the Westminster Parliament. In a federal constitution, any powers not specified in the constitution automatically fall to regional institutions.

Examples: unitary constitutions: UK, France, Italy; federal constitutions: USA, Germany, India.

> **Unitary/federal constitutions** refer to a classification of constitutions into two types. Unitary constitutions are where sovereignty or ultimate power lies in one central body. In federal constitutions, sovereignty is divided between the central authority and other, regional bodies such as US states or provinces.

What are the sources of the UK constitution?

Because the UK constitution is not codified, it has a number of different sources. Table 5.1 shows the types of source, describes each type and gives some important examples of each.

Table 5.1 Sources of the UK constitution

Type of source	Description of source	Examples
Parliamentary statutes	These are laws, passed by the UK Parliament, which have a constitutional effect.	• The Human Rights Act 1998 brought the European Convention on Human Rights into UK law. • The Scotland Act 1998 transferred considerable power to a Scottish Parliament. • The Freedom of Information Act 2000 gave considerable public access to official documents and information.

(Continued)

Table 5.1 Sources of the UK constitution (*continued*)

Type of source	Description of source	Examples
Conventions	These are rules that are not legally enforceable, but which are considered binding and so are *virtually* laws.	• The Salisbury Convention is a rule that the House of Lords cannot obstruct a proposal that was contained in the governing party's last election manifesto. • Collective cabinet responsibility states that members of the government should always defend all government policies.
Common law	Similar to conventions, these are unwritten laws, but unlike conventions, they can be enforced by the courts.	• The use of prerogative powers by the prime minister results from common law. This means the prime minister has a range of powers, transferred from the monarchy, but not sanctioned by Parliament. • Many individual rights and freedoms are established by common law.
European Union treaties	The UK has signed a number of treaties, mostly concerning the transfer of power and sovereignty from the UK to the EU.	• The Maastricht Treaty of 1992 and Lisbon (Reform) Treaty of 2007 both transferred power from the UK to the EU.
Works of authority	These are the writings of constitutional experts which describe constitutional practice. They have so much authority that they have become part of the constitution.	• The rule of law as described by nineteenth-century constitutional expert, A. V. Dicey, establishes the principle of equality under the law. • The 2010 O'Donnell Rules were written by the Cabinet Secretary as a guide to how to form a government with a hung parliament.
Traditions	These are customs and practices that have grown up over a long period of time. They are not legal, but tend to persist.	• The annual Queen's Speech is how the government's annual legislative programme is announced. • Parliamentary procedures are largely traditional.

Now test yourself

2 Give two examples of each of the following:

(a) Constitutional conventions

(b) Books of constitutional authority

(c) Constitutional statutes

(d) EU treaties

Answers on p. 107

Tested

What are the main features of the UK constitution?

Revised

This section identifies the main distinguishing features of the UK constitution:

● It is not codified. This makes it very flexible and certainly not entrenched.

● Constitutional laws are not superior to other laws.

● The sovereignty of Parliament is fundamental. This means that, ultimately, the constitution and its rules are in the control of

Parliament. It means that constitutional rules cannot be entrenched and that Parliament can amend the constitution at will.

- There is a constitutional monarchy. The queen is head of state but is constitutionally limited so that her powers are held in reserve and not expected to be used in normal circumstances.
- The rule of law operates. All are equal under the law and the government itself is subject to laws, just as citizens are.
- It is unitary. This means that all sovereignty, ultimate power, lies with the UK Parliament.
- There is a lack of separation of powers. This means that the executive and legislative branches are not separated from each other and that the executive (government) dominates the legislature (Parliament).

Sovereignty and the constitution

Where does sovereignty lie in the British system?

Revised

This is a difficult question as the concept of sovereignty is uncertain. However, the following assertions can be made:

- Parliament is legally sovereign. This means it is the ultimate source of law and the ultimate source of all political power.
- UK government shares this sovereignty to some extent because it has the people's mandate to implement its political programme. This means Parliament should not normally defy the will of the government when it is acting within the people's mandate.
- The people are sovereign at elections.
- Referendums do not grant sovereignty to the people because they are not binding on Parliament. However, referendum results are sovereign *in practice.*
- The European Union has legal sovereignty in those areas where it has jurisdiction. However, the UK has not given up sovereignty finally to the EU because it can leave and regain all its sovereignty.
- The devolved administrations do not have legal sovereignty, but they have *quasi* sovereignty. This means that the power granted to them is unlikely ever to return to Westminster.

> **Parliamentary sovereignty** is a principle, fundamental to the British political system, that legal sovereignty lies with Parliament and that Parliament is the ultimate source of all political power.
>
> **Quasi federalism** is an expression which suggests that the devolution process looks effectively like federalism, but is not federalism specifically because no sovereignty has been divided.

Typical mistake

Students of politics often confuse sovereignty and power, and tend to use the terms interchangeably. This is a mistake. Sovereignty means ultimate power which cannot be overruled. Power is a weaker expression in that it can be taken away if the sovereign parliament wishes to. Be careful which expression you use.

Examiner's tip

When discussing the location of sovereignty in the UK, it is important to demonstrate that it is constantly shifting between government and Parliament, between the UK and the EU, and towards the people through referendums.

Now test yourself

3   What is being described in each of these cases?
   (a) It is an elected body that can make laws and appears to be legally sovereign but is not legally sovereign.
   (b) It is a regular occurrence that makes the people temporarily sovereign.
   (c) It is an institution that has some legal sovereignty in the UK, but the UK can take it back.
   (d) It is a body that shares legal sovereignty with Parliament.
   (e) It is a way of making people sovereign other than an election.

Answers on p. 107

How has sovereignty in the UK changed since 1997?

Revised ✓

Although legal sovereignty undoubtedly lies with the UK Parliament, sovereignty in a more general sense has moved. These are the ways it has changed since Labour began to reform the constitution in 1997:

● A great deal of political sovereignty has been transferred to devolved administrations.

● More sovereignty has been transferred to the European Union.

● There has been an increasing use of referendums to resolve key issues.

● Arguably the power of the executive in relation to Parliament has grown, giving it effectively more sovereignty.

● It has been argued that the incorporation of the European Convention on Human Rights into UK law is *effectively* a transfer of sovereignty over civil liberties.

> **Examiner's tip**
>
> Examiners often ask whether parliamentary sovereignty is a reality or a myth. You should be well prepared for this discussion.

The European Union and the UK constitution

Revised ✓

What has been the impact of membership of the EU on the constitution?

The UK joined the EU in 1973, since when large amounts of sovereignty have been transferred to Europe — a process sometimes known as 'pooling sovereignty'. The impacts of EU membership have been as follows:

● EU laws are superior to UK laws.

● In any conflict between EU law and UK law, EU law prevails.

● UK courts must enforce EU law.

● Appeals based on EU law are heard in senior British courts, but final appeals may go to the European Court of Justice.

● Parliament has surrendered sovereignty to the EU in certain specific policy areas, as defined in a series of treaties. In these areas, sovereignty is pooled.

● Areas of pooled sovereignty include trade, consumer law, employment law, agricultural subsidies and fishing regulation.

● Parliamentary sovereignty has not been permanently lost as the UK can leave the EU.

> **Pooled sovereignty** is a term used to describe how legal sovereignty within the European Union is shared among its members.

Reforming the constitution

Should the UK constitution be codified?

This question refers to the long-running debate over whether it is time to codify the UK constitution. This is an argument that is usually promoted by liberals, mainly on the basis that Britain's constitutional arrangements are now out of debate. Table 5.2 summarises the debate.

Typical mistake

It is wrong to say the UK constitution is *unwritten*. In fact, most of it today *is* written. The key point is that it is not *codified*: that is, written in a single document or source. Be careful not to write 'unwritten' when you mean 'uncodified'.

Table 5.2 The codification debate

In favour of codification	Against codification
• **Clarity.** Citizens know how power is distributed and what the limits are to the power of political institutions.	• **Flexibility.** An uncodified constitution can be easily changed and so evolve and adapt to changing circumstances.
• **Limiting government.** A codified constitution is likely to prevent a 'drift' of power towards over-powerful government.	• **Strong government.** A codified constitution might limit the power of government too much, making government ineffective.
• **Safeguarding the constitution.** If codified, it would be difficult for a short-term government to amend the constitution for its own, narrow, benefit.	• **Accountability.** Governments cannot 'hide' behind an uncodified constitution to justify their inactivity, thus making them more accountable.
• **Rights.** A codified constitution would clearly state the rights of citizens and help prevent government from abusing those rights.	• **Popular control.** Though uncodified constitutions seem easy to change, in practice they can only be changed if the people desire change. So the constitution is more under popular control.
• **Strong judiciability.** Such a constitution could be effectively protected by the senior judges.	• **Weak judiciability.** As it is not codified, such a constitution is less subject to control by unelected, unaccountable judges.

The reforms under Labour after 1997

This section details the constitutional reforms made by the Labour government after it came to power in 1997.

Devolution

Considerable powers were transferred to a Scottish Parliament, Welsh Assembly and Northern Ireland Assembly. The process was known as **devolution**.

Elected mayors

An elected mayor was introduced for Greater London. Referendums in other parts of the country resulted in 11 further examples of elected mayors.

> **Devolution** is a process of transferring power from the UK Parliament and government to regional governments in Scotland, Wales and Northern Ireland. This does not represent any transfer of sovereignty.

The Human Rights Act

The European Convention on Human Rights became part of British law, binding on all bodies other than the UK Parliament.

Freedom of information

An Act gave citizens the right to view information being held about themselves as well as public records and documents. These had previously been unobtainable.

House of Lords reform

All but 92 of the hereditary peers lost their voting rights in the Lords. A new Appointments Commission was set up to regulate the appointment of future peers.

Electoral reform

Proposals to hold a referendum on electoral reform for general elections were dropped. However, proportional electoral systems were introduced for devolved elections in Scotland, Wales and Northern Ireland.

Judicial reform

The highest court of appeal, effectively the constitutional court, was transferred away from the senior judges sitting in the House of Lords, to a new Supreme Court. This was to make the senior judiciary more independent. The legal system was removed from control by the Lord Chancellor and a new Judicial Appointments Commission was set up to ensure judicial independence.

> **Examiner's tip**
>
> Examiners are looking not just for *how* the UK constitution has been reformed, but also for *why* and *how effectively?*

Why did Labour reform the constitution?   Revised

Labour was keen to reform the constitution for a number of reasons:

- **Modernisation.** The constitution looked out of date and out of step with the rest of Europe. New Labour was a modernising party.
- **Electoral advantage.** Labour believed electoral reform would be popular and help it win votes, especially in Scotland and Wales.
- **Democratisation.** New Labour was influenced by liberalism and so wished to make the constitution more democratic and liberal in nature.
- **Anti-conservatism.** Conservatives opposed reform, which was a reason for Labour to defy them. Labour also believed there had been a drift towards excessive executive power under the Conservatives since 1979.

Coalition proposals to reform the constitution   Revised

The coalition government elected in 2010 proposed a number of constitutional reforms, as detailed in Table 5.3.

Exam practice answers and quick quizzes at **www.therevisionbutton.co.uk/myrevisionnotes**

Table 5.3 Coalition constitutional reform proposals

Proposal	Detail
Electoral reform	A referendum was to be held in May 2011 on whether to introduce the alternative vote system for general elections. The referendum voted 'No'.
Fixed-term parliaments	These were agreed in 2010. The gap between elections to the House of Commons was fixed at 5 years. This took away the prime minister's power to determine the date of general elections.
House of Lords reform	Legislation was to be introduced to create a partly or fully elected House of Lords.
A British Bill of Rights	Consideration was to be given to replacing the Human Rights Act with a British Bill of Rights outside the control of the European Court of Human Rights.
Equal constituency sizes	In 2011, legislation began the process of redrawing constituency boundaries to ensure all parliamentary constituencies are of equal size.
Recall of MPs	Constituents were to have the power to hold a vote on whether to 'recall' MPs who abuse their position.
Devolution	Promise of a Welsh referendum on more power to its assembly was to be honoured (a 'yes' vote was achieved in February 2011). Promise to allow a Scottish referendum on increased powers to the Scottish Government and Parliament.
European Union	Any proposed transfer of sovereignty to the European Union could only take place following a 'yes' vote in a referendum.
Elected mayors	Referendums were to be held in major cities to determine whether they should introduce elected mayors (if there was not already one in existence).

Now test yourself

Tested

4 Look at each of these constitutional developments. In each case, describe a constitutional reform (implemented or proposed since 1997) designed to create them.
   (a) Better safeguards for human rights
   (b) Establishing autonomous regional government
   (c) Improving the legitimacy of part of Parliament
   (d) Taking away the prime minister's power to manipulate the date of a general election for his party's own ends
   (e) Establishing a more independent body at the head of the judiciary
   (f) Making government more open
   (g) Establishing fairer voting systems
   (h) Making constituency representation fairer

Answers on p. 107

Evaluating constitutional reform

Revised

This section considers the extent to which the constitution has been reformed as well as the ways in which reform has *not* taken place.

Examiner's tip

It is important for students to keep up to date with constitutional reform. Examiners look for up-to-date knowledge.

Key changes

- Government has been decentralised through devolution and the introduction of elected mayors.
- Rights are better protected though the Human Rights Act and the Freedom of Information Act.
- The House of Lords has, arguably, become a more effective check on the power of government.
- The electoral systems of Scotland, Wales and Northern Ireland have been made more proportional.
- The judiciary is more independent, making it more able to protect rights and check abuses of governmental power.
- The introduction of fixed terms means that governments cannot manipulate election dates for their own advantage.
- The proposals for reforming constituency boundaries and introducing recall of MPs may make them more accountable.

Criticisms and failed reforms

- It can be argued that the United Kingdom has been weakened by devolution.
- The Human Rights Act and greater judicial independence have created conflict between senior judges and government.
- Parliamentary sovereignty means that rights cannot properly be protected.
- Electoral reform has failed.
- The future of House of Lords reform is uncertain and the Lords remains an undemocratic institution.
- Many argue that the UK still needs a codified constitution.
- It is argued that the executive remains too strong and Parliament too weak.

Strengths and weaknesses of the UK constitution

Revised

The UK constitution has been both praised and criticised. Table 5.4 evaluates the current UK constitution.

> **Elective dictatorship** is a description of how the executive (government) branch in the British political system is dominant to such an extent that it has been described as a 'dictatorship'.

Typical mistake

The term 'elective dictatorship' is often used to describe the British political system. This is often accurate, but there are times when government is very strong in relation to Parliament, and other times when it is relatively weak. It is a mistake to describe the executive branch as *always* dominant. It is, however, *often* dominant.

Exam practice answers and quick quizzes at **www.therevisionbutton.co.uk/myrevisionnotes**

Table 5.4 The UK constitution evaluated

Positive elements	Negative elements
• It is flexible. Because it is uncodified, it can evolve naturally and respond easily to changing circumstances.	• It is too flexible and so can be amended by a temporary government that wishes to serve its own purposes.
• It provides for strong, decisive government which is not constrained by constitutional rules. The government's mandate is normally clear.	• It allows governments to have too much power, as there are inadequate constitutional safeguards in place.
• It has stood the test of time and so remains part of Britain's political traditions.	• It is old fashioned and does not conform to the normal picture of a modern constitution. It allows for undemocratic institutions such as the House of Lords and the monarchy.
• The doctrine of parliamentary sovereignty makes government relatively accountable.	• Parliament is too weak relative to government and it is insufficiently representative. The electoral system reinforces the lack of representation.
• Its unitary nature helps to maintain national unity.	• Power is much too centralised and so threatens democracy.
• The independent judiciary ensures the rule of law is maintained.	• Individual rights are not well protected because Parliament is not subject to constitutional control.
• It provides for a collective form of government, as opposed to presidential systems which may place too much power in the hands of one individual.	• The fact that it is not codified means that citizens find it difficult to understand.

Check your understanding

Tested ☐

1 Identify three sources of the UK constitution.
2 Name three functions of a constitution.
3 Identify three important features of the UK constitution.
4 Identify three constitutional reforms made between 1997 and 2009.
5 Identify three constitutional reforms made from 2010 onwards.
6 Describe a unitary constitution.
7 Describe a federal constitution.

Answers on p. 107

Exam practice

Source questions

Read the passage and answer the questions that follow.

The UK constitution has been reformed since 1997 to a greater extent than ever in its long history. The Labour programme of post-1997 was designed to modernise the constitution, as well as making it more democratic, accessible and capable of responding to demands for more openness in government and better protection of civil liberties. Devolution introduced autonomous regional government, while the Human Rights Act established a codified set of rights for UK citizens. The more recent introduction of the Supreme Court has made the judiciary more independent and therefore even more capable of protecting our rights. Though the pace of change has slowed, the 2010 coalition has proposed further reform. Fixed-term parliaments have been established and a serious attempt is being made to reform the House of Lords, creating a partly elected second chamber. Nevertheless the potentially most far-reaching reform — the use of the alternative vote for general elections — was rejected in a referendum in 2011.

1 With reference to the source, identify two constitutional reforms together with how they were designed to improve the constitution. [5]

2 With reference to the source and your own knowledge, explain how the reforms have created better protection of rights in the UK. [10]

3 How and to what extent does the UK constitution remain undemocratic? [25]

Essay questions

4 Assess the arguments in favour of introducing a codified constitution in the UK. [40]

5 To what extent is the UK constitution outdated? [40]

6 How, and to what extent, has parliamentary sovereignty been eroded in the UK? [40]

7 How successful has constitutional reform been since 1997? [40]

Answers and quick quiz 5 online

Online

Examiner's summary

✓ Constitutions are key elements in a country's political system. They determine the distribution of power and the relationships between political institutions. They are also key documents for establishing citizens' rights.

✓ The UK constitution is unusual for a number of reasons. First, it is not codified, and secondly it is largely replaced by the doctrine of parliamentary sovereignty. This means that Parliament has control of the constitution and can change it at will. It also makes the constitution highly flexible. However, it does not mean that there is no such thing as the UK constitution.

✓ The UK constitution has a number of different sources including statutes, conventions, common law, EU treaties, traditions and works of constitutional authority.

✓ Sovereignty is a key idea in constitutional matters. It means ultimate legal power and the ultimate source of all political power. Parliament is legally sovereign in the UK. However, sovereignty can also be said to reside with the people in elections or referendums. It can also be said to lie with government because of its electoral mandate. The EU has sovereignty in areas of its jurisdiction. Devolution

has conferred a kind of quasi sovereignty on devolved administrations.

✓ The location of sovereignty in the UK is constantly shifting as political circumstances change.

✓ Membership of the EU has had major impacts on the EU's constitutional arrangements.

✓ A key question of British politics is whether or not the constitution should be codified.

✓ Constitutions are either unitary, where sovereignty lies in one central place, or federal, where sovereignty is divided between the centre and regions.

✓ Major reform of the UK constitution began in 1997 with the advent of a Labour government. A further round of reform is proposed by the coalition government that took power in 2010.

✓ Reform of the constitution has certainly improved democracy and rights in the UK, and has also decentralised power through devolution. Many critics, however, argue that there is much to be done to modernise and democratise the UK.

6 Parliament

The UK Parliament stands at the centre of the British political system. This is because it is the source of all political power and is legally sovereign. The government has to be drawn from Parliament and the government is accountable to Parliament. The reform of Parliament has been a major political issue since 2010 with proposals for the reform of both Houses.

Legislatures and executives

The nature of Parliament
Revised

Parliament is bicameral, meaning it has two chambers with distinctive memberships and functions. These are described below.

House of Commons

The House of Commons has the following features:

- It is made up of 650 MPs elected in constituencies.
- MPs represent the interests of their constituents and constituencies.
- The majority (either a single party or coalition) in the Commons forms the government.
- Members of the government make up the government front bench.
- The senior members of other parties make up the opposition front benches.
- MPs not on the front benches are known as backbenchers.
- There are departmental and other select committees that question ministers, civil servants, officials and other representatives with a view to investigating and evaluating the work of government departments.
- There are legislative committees that look at proposed legislation with a view to improving it through amendments.
- Each party in Parliament has whips who inform members about business, maintain party discipline and act as channels of communication between party leaderships and backbench MPs.
- The government front bench controls most of the parliamentary agenda.
- A neutral 'Speaker' presides over its proceedings.

> **Bicameralism** describes a situation where a parliament has two chambers. The UK is bicameral.
>
> **Parliament** is also known as the legislature. A parliament is a body that has several roles, including legitimising legislation, passing laws, scrutinising and amending legislation, calling government to account, representing voters and other groups, and controlling governmental power. The UK Parliament has sovereignty — ultimate power. The Scottish Parliament performs a similar role in Scotland but is not sovereign.

> **Typical mistake**
>
> It is very common for exam candidates, when asked about Parliament, to consider only the House of Commons. If the question refers to 'Parliament', consider both the Commons and the Lords.

> **Typical mistake**
>
> Many students mix up ministers and MPs. This is probably because they know that ministers are also MPs as they also sit for a constituency. However, it is very important to distinguish between the role of ministers who are part of the government, and MPs who represent constituencies, even though the same person may perform both functions.

House of Lords

The House of Lords has the following features:

- The House of Lords is known as the 'upper house', but is actually the junior partner of the Commons.
- Its membership consists of 92 hereditary peers who have inherited their title, 26 archbishops and bishops of the Church of England, and several hundred life peers who have the right to sit in the Lords for their whole lives.
- The Lords has legislative committees but not departmental select committees.
- As well as party members, the Lords contains 'crossbenchers' who are not affiliated to any party and so are highly independent.
- No one party has a majority in the Lords.
- A neutral 'Lord Speaker' presides over its proceedings.

Typical mistake

The House of Lords is often described as an unelected, over-aged and outdated institution. This may be so, but it also contains many dedicated legislators, whose average age is steadily falling and many of whom have a wealth of expertise and experience.

The functions of Parliament

Revised

Accountability is the device whereby the government is accountable to Parliament, meaning it must make itself available for criticism and must justify its policies to Parliament. Ultimately, the government may be removed by Parliament. Accountability can also refer to the fact that elected representatives are answerable to their electorates.

The **Westminster model** is a description of the British central political system, which is used more rarely today. It describes the fact that Parliament is the central representative body, that all power flows from Parliament and that the government is accountable to Parliament. It also means that members of the government have to be drawn from Parliament.

Typical mistake

It is a common mistake to believe that the main role of Parliament is to obstruct and control the government. This is not so. Parliament should only be obstructive when the government is seen to be abusing its power, not acting in the public interest or exceeding its mandate. The main role of Parliament is to support the government and to legitimise its proposals.

Joint functions of both Houses

The following functions are carried out jointly by the Commons and the Lords:

- granting formal approval for legislation
- calling government to account
- scrutinising legislation and proposing amendments
- debating key political issues

Functions of the Commons

The following functions are carried out only by the Commons:

- representing constituencies and constituents
- MPs may seek the redress of grievances of citizens and groups
- vetoing legislation in extreme circumstances when it is considered against the national interest
- removing a government from power if it has lost its legitimacy

Functions of the Lords

The following functions are carried out only by the Lords:

- delaying legislation for at least a year in order to force government to reconsider it
- representing various interests and causes in society
- proposing amendments to legislation in order to improve it and protect minority interests

What is parliamentary government?

In parliamentary government:

- There is no separation of powers between the government and Parliament.
- Government draws its authority from Parliament, not directly from the people.
- Government is not separately elected from Parliament.
- Government is accountable directly to Parliament.
- Members of the government must sit in the legislature.

What is presidential government?

In presidential government:

- The executive and legislative branches of government are separate.
- The president is elected separately from the legislature.
- The president does not sit in the legislature.
- The president is accountable to the people, not the legislature.
- There are constitutional rules that establish the limits of the president's powers.

Now test yourself

1 Briefly describe five differences in the composition or functions of the Lords and the Commons.

Answers on p. 107

Tested

> **Representative and responsible government** is a description of the British polity which simply suggests that the people are represented by both Parliament and government, and that government is constantly held responsible for its actions by Parliament.

Government and Parliament

Revised

> **Separation of powers** is the principle that the powers of the executive and the legislature should be firmly separated. This is in order that they can control each other's power though a system of checks and balances. There is no such separation of powers in the UK.
>
> **Fusion of powers** is in many ways the opposite of the separation of powers. It means that there is overlap between the executive and the legislature. In practice the executive (government) dominates the legislature (Parliament). It also means that members of the government are also members of Parliament.

Reasons why the government dominates Parliament

It is normally stressed that the executive branch in the UK (the government) dominates Parliament. There are a number of reasons why this may be so:

- The government can claim a mandate from the people for its policies when it is elected to power. Parliament, therefore, lacks the legitimate right to ignore the mandate and tends to accept the government's right to govern.
- Governments normally enjoy a clear majority of support in the Commons (the 2010 election was an exception, but a majority

coalition was formed·instead of a one-party majority). This means the government can normally count on the majority of support.

- The MPs of the governing party were elected on the understanding that they would help to implement the party manifesto. On the whole, therefore, the MPs of the governing majority will normally support the government.

- Party loyalty is strong in the UK compared to many other democracies.

- Patronage is a key factor. Most MPs seek promotion to government at some time. By remaining loyal they improve their chances of promotion. All government posts are in the hands of the prime minister, so he or she exercises a great deal of influence over ambitious MPs. This is known as the 'power of patronage'.

- Governments (as well as opposition parties) use whips, who are senior MPs, to maintain party discipline and to remind MPs where their first loyalty lies. Rebellious MPs receive warnings and then may suffer suspension from their party.

- The House of Lords' influence is limited by statute and convention. The Parliament Act 1949 limits the House of Lords to only being able to delay legislation for 1 year. It cannot block government proposals permanently. Any amendments to legislation must also be approved by the Commons, where the government enjoys a majority. Furthermore, the Lords has no power to interfere in financial matters (under the earlier 1911 Parliament Act). The Salisbury convention is considered to be binding and states that the House of Lords must not obstruct any government proposal that was contained in its most recent election manifesto. In other words, the unelected Lords must not defy the will of the elected government.

Ways in which Parliament can control the government

On the other hand, government does not have it all its own way. Parliament can control government in a number of ways:

- Ultimately Parliament is sovereign. This means it can veto legislation if it believes it is not in the public interest and/or the government has no legitimate mandate for the proposal.

- In extreme circumstances the House of Commons can remove a government through a vote of no confidence.

- Parliament has the power to amend legislation to improve it or remove offending clauses.

- Governments cannot hope to override significant parliamentary opposition to a proposal.

- The House of Lords retains independence because there is no government majority there and patronage is weaker. It can therefore defy the will of government.

- MPs and peers can call government to account publicly.

- Powerful departmental select committees can be, and have been, critical of government.

Table 6.1 gives some examples of occasions when Parliament has defied government.

Exam practice answers and quick quizzes at **www.therevisionbutton.co.uk/myrevisionnotes**

Table 6.1 Major examples of Parliament defying the will of the government

Occasion	Detail
1979 vote of no confidence	The Labour government under prime minister James Callaghan was removed prematurely from office after a sustained period of industrial unrest and economic problems.
1986 Shops Bill	The only time in Margaret Thatcher's period in office that her government lost a vote on a major piece of legislation. The Shops Bill was a proposal to allow more shops to open for trading on a Sunday. The government underestimated the strength of opposition within the Conservative Party.
1994 VAT rise defeated	John Major's government was defeated in the Commons over a proposal to raise the rate of VAT on fuel and energy.
2005 detention of terrorist suspects	Tony Blair's attempt to extend the period that terrorist suspects could be held for questioning without trial to 90 days was defeated in the House of Commons.
2008 detention of terrorist suspects	Gordon Brown's attempt to extend the period of detention to 42 days was defeated in the House of Lords and the government did not attempt to overturn it.
2011 Fixed Term Parliaments Bill defeated	The House of Lords defeated the coalition government on the provision to introduce 5-year fixed parliamentary terms permanently. It insisted that the measure would lapse after 2015 unless renewed by Parliament.

Examiner's tip

As with most questions, it is crucial to include examples to illustrate your response. For example, when discussing the relationship between government and Parliament, it is important to include examples of when Parliament has defied the will of the government.

Now test yourself

Tested ☐

2 Identify **three** reasons why the government tends to dominate Parliament and **three** ways in which Parliament can control the government.

Answers on p. 108

Parliamentary committees

Revised ☐

Much of the work of Parliament is conducted in committees. The main committees are shown below, together with their work and status.

Departmental select committees

Departmental select committees in the House of Commons:

- normally consist of 11–13 backbench MPs
- oversee the work of government departments
- can question ministers, civil servants, advisers and other witnesses or call for official papers
- produce reports that are often unanimous and cross party lines
- have often been critical of government's work and are influential

Public Accounts Committee

The Public Accounts Committee (PAC) in the House of Commons:

- is always chaired by an opposition backbencher
- investigates the financial aspects of government
- is highly influential and often critical

Legislative committees

Legislative committees of the House of Commons:

- usually consist of 15–40 backbench MPs
- consider possible amendments to proposed legislation
- always have a government majority
- rarely pass amendments against government wishes
- are seen as largely ineffectual except where an issue is not controversial between the parties

Legislative Committees of the House of Lords:

- contain 15+ members
- often contain peers who are experts on the issue being legislated
- are subject to weaker party discipline than in the Commons
- often pass significant amendments to improve legislation and/or protect minorities
- often defy the government's wishes
- make amendments that are subject to approval in the Commons, so their power is weakened
- do sometimes force the government to change its mind

Role of Parliament

Evaluation of the House of Commons   Revised

This section considers how effectively the House of Commons carries out its roles. The evaluation is best considered in terms of each of those roles in turn.

Representation

- **Positive:** Most MPs are very active in representing the interests of their constituency and of individual constituents. Many MPs also represent the interests of large associations and pressure groups.
- **Negative:** The Commons is not socially representative. There are a minority of women and few representatives from minority ethnic groups or from smaller religions. The members are predominantly middle class and from a background in the professions. Party loyalty also means they tend to toe the party line rather than always representing the national interest or group interests. The worst aspect is that the party make-up of the Commons does not accurately represent support for the parties among the electorate. Large parties tend to be over-represented, while small parties are under-represented. This is the result of the first-past-the-post electoral system.

Calling government to account

- **Positive:** MPs regularly question ministers at question time sessions. The Liaison Committee also questions the prime minister twice a

Examiner's tip

When examiners ask for an evaluation of Parliament's effectiveness, they expect to see such an evaluation with respect to Parliament's expected functions. In other words, when analysing the effectiveness of Parliament, it is best to look at each of its main functions and evaluate its performance of each in turn.

Exam practice answers and quick quizzes at **www.therevisionbutton.co.uk/myrevisionnotes**

year. Ministers are forced, by tradition, to present all policies to the Commons before any other public announcements. The departmental select committees are extremely active and independent. They examine government business closely and are often critical to good effect.

- **Negative:** Prime Minister's Question Time (PMQT) has become something of a media sideshow with little relevance to real policy examination. Many MPs are also reluctant to be critical of ministers of their own party for fear of being seen as disloyal.

Scrutiny

- **Positive:** The departmental select committees have proved very effective in scrutinising the policies of government departments and publicising shortcomings or failures.
- **Negative:** MPs are given relatively little time to scrutinise proposed legislation, so laws are often poorly drafted. Because the legislative committees are whipped into party loyalty, MPs are not independent-minded in their scrutiny function.

Legislating

- **Positive:** It is a key role of the Commons to make legislation *legitimate*. This effectively means granting consent on behalf of the people. On the whole this operates well and the laws are generally respected because they have been legitimised in Parliament. The Commons does retain the power to block legislation that is against the public interest or represents an abuse of power.
- **Negative:** The procedures of Parliament in respect of passing legislation are ancient and considered to be inefficient and ritualised.

Deliberation

- **Positive:** From time to time the Commons is seen at its best in debates on the great issues of the day: for example, on the war in Iraq, over how to deal with terrorism and on the funding of higher education.
- **Negative:** The Commons is given relatively little time for debate on legislation itself, so crowded is its programme. Furthermore, debates on legislative proposals tend to divide along party lines and so lose their authority.

Checking government power

- **Positive:** The Commons retains the power to veto legislation and this represents a discipline upon governments.
- **Negative:** Party loyalty and discipline means that many MPs are reluctant to challenge the government. The government very rarely loses a major vote in the Commons.

Evaluation of the House of Lords Revised

This section considers how effectively the House of Lords carries out its roles. The evaluation is best considered in terms of each of those roles in turn.

Representation

- **Positive:** In many ways the Lords is more representative than the Commons. Many sections of society and associations are represented by peers who have special links with them and specific experience and knowledge.
- **Negative:** The Lords is unelected and so could be said to represent no one because it is not accountable. It is not socially representative, with a high average age, a shortage of women and ethnic minority members, and few members from working-class origins.

Calling government to account

- **Positive:** Peers are more independent-minded than MPs, so they can be more active in their questioning and criticisms of ministers.
- **Negative:** There are no departmental select committees in the Lords, so a valuable means by which government can be called to account is missing.

Scrutiny

- **Positive:** The legislative committees in the Lords can be more effective than their counterparts in the Commons. These committees divide much less along party lines and are more independent. Furthermore, the peers who are members often have special knowledge, expertise and experience in the matters contained in the legislation.
- **Negative:** Though the Lords often does propose legislative amendments, it cannot force them through as they may be overturned by the Commons.

Legislating

- **Positive:** Laws must be passed through the Lords to legitimate them. People can be confident that legislation has been fully scrutinised.
- **Negative:** As an unelected body, the Lords cannot provide legitimation to legislation.

Deliberation

- **Positive:** The Lords has two great advantages in deliberating on important issues. First, it has more time to do so than the Commons. Secondly, the Lords contains a vast well of knowledge and experience among its members.
- **Negative:** The fact that the Lords has very weak legislating powers means that its debates may be largely symbolic.

Checking government power

- **Positive:** As the government cannot control members of the Lords, the House does, from time to time, act in a very independent way.
- **Negative:** Ultimately the government has several ways of by-passing obstruction by the Lords. The elected government and House of Commons will win out over the unelected Lords.

Exam practice answers and quick quizzes at **www.therevisionbutton.co.uk/myrevisionnotes**

Now test yourself

3 Look at each of the characteristics of Parliament's relationship with the government. In each case, tick the appropriate column to say whether they are factors that give the government dominance or that help Parliament to control the government:

Feature	Help government?	Help Parliament?
There is strong party loyalty		
MPs have strong constituency links		
Votes of no confidence		
Departmental select committees		
MPs' research capability		
Party whips		
The Parliament Act 1949		
Legislative committees in the Commons		
Legislative committees in the Lords		
Crossbenchers in the Lords		
Political patronage		

Answers on p. 108

How effective are MPs and peers?

Table 6.2 is an evaluation of the work of MPs and peers in terms of the functions of Parliament.

Table 6.2 Evaluation of parliamentary representatives

Positives	Negatives
MPs	
• They strongly represent the interests and grievances of constituents and constituencies. • Departmental select committees staffed by backbenchers have a good reputation for calling government to account. • MPs can be effective when questioning ministers on the floor of the House. • Some independent-minded, campaigning MPs can work effectively on behalf of pressure groups and political campaigns.	• When there is a conflict between party policy and constituency interest, party policy often wins. • MPs on legislative committees are ineffective because the government dominates them and whips enforce strict party discipline. • Whips enforce strict party discipline on all key debates and votes. • MPs have little in the way of research resources and administrative back-up to help them. • Little time is reserved in Parliament for backbench business.
Peers	
• Peers are more independent of party control and so can be more effective as individuals. • Many are experts in particular areas of policy and so can help to improve legislation and the quality of debate. • Many campaigning peers do effective work on behalf of pressure groups. • Peers do not have to fight elections and may hold office for long periods, giving them continuity. They also have no constituency duties, which frees up their time.	• Peers are paid little and have a minimum of research and administrative back-up. • The powers of the House of Lords are limited. It is the junior House. • As they are not elected, peers lack democratic legitimacy and so have less authority. • They are not professional politicians and so may find it difficult to access the political system.

The impact of EU membership on Parliament

The following effects of EU membership can be identified:

- EU law is superior to UK law.
- UK laws cannot contradict EU law. Parliament must take this into account.
- Some areas of policy have been taken out of Parliament's hands.
- Parliament has developed committees to study proposed legislation from the EU, but they have limited influence.
- Consideration of European legislation happens more in the Lords than the Commons because the Lords has more time and expertise available.
- Parliamentary sovereignty does mean that the UK could leave the EU at any time.

Reform of Parliament

Since 1997 the issue of parliamentary reform has been high on the political agenda. Until 2010 attention tended to focus on the House of Lords, though progress remained limited. After 2010 attention shifted to the House of Commons, though Lords reform remained a prominent issue.

Examiner's tip

The key issue in relation to Parliament and its reform is *legitimacy*. Examiners will be looking for strong analysis of how the legitimacy of both the Commons and the Lords will be affected by their reform.

Reform of the House of Commons

In 2010 two reforms were introduced and the coalition government produced proposals for a further four.

The 2010 reforms

The 2010 reforms were as follows:

- In June 2010 the Backbench Business Committee was set up with a chair elected by MPs. The committee controls the debates in the main chamber on 27 days per year and may select any topic. Topics in 2010 included the war in Afghanistan and the concept of the 'Big Society'. It also schedules 8 days of debate in Westminster Central Hall.
- From 2010 onwards the chairs of the departmental select committees are elected by backbench MPs. This takes that power away from the party whips and leaders.

The 2010 proposed reforms

The reforms proposed in 2010 were:

- A House of Commons Business Committee is to be set up. This will control the business of the House virtually completely.

Exam practice answers and quick quizzes at **www.therevisionbutton.co.uk/myrevisionnotes**

- The constituency boundaries are to be redrawn to make them of equal size. In this way it is believed that elections will be fairer and MPs will have equal responsibilities.
- Constituents are to be given the power to recall their MPs if they feel there has been an abuse of power or other misconduct. Effectively a petition can force a by-election at which the sitting MP will be forced to seek re-election.
- The size of the House is to be reduced by 10%. This is partly a money-saving measure but it will also slightly streamline the Commons.

Why were these reforms proposed?

- There was widespread disillusionment with politicians, and MPs in particular. The reforms were partly designed to restore respect.
- To make the House of Commons more accountable.
- To improve the ability of backbench MPs to call the government to account.
- To make voting power in constituencies more equal.

> **Examiner's tip**
>
> Students must bring themselves up to date on which reforms have actually been implemented.

Reform of the House of Lords

Revised

The Lords was last reformed in 1999. In that year all but 92 of the hereditary peers lost their attendance and voting rights.

By the time of the 2010 general election, all three main parties were committed to further reform. Proposals were included in the coalition agreement between the Conservatives and Liberal Democrats.

The options for reform have been these:

- **Complete abolition of the second chamber:** a view once held by many left-wing socialist MPs. They argued that there is no need for a second chamber of any kind.
- **A completely appointed second chamber:** a view held largely within the Conservative Party. It is attractive because it would bring a large number of 'worthy' people into politics and would be a very independent chamber, as its members would not rely on the support of political parties.
- **A completely elected second chamber:** a proposal supported by all Liberal Democrats, most Labour members and many Conservatives. Its supporters argue that it is the most democratic solution and would provide an effective, legitimate check on the power of government.
- **A partly elected, partly appointed second chamber:** a proposal supported by some Conservatives and Labour members. Proposals for the combination range from 50%–50% to 80% elected, 20% appointed.

These options are considered further in Table 6.3 overleaf.

> **Typical mistake**
>
> The Labour government's 1999 reform of the House of Lords, reducing the number of hereditary peers to 92, might seem a merely 'cosmetic exercise'. It is a mistake to think this. Although it appeared a minor reform, it had quite a dramatic effect, making the Lords more legitimate and influencing them to become more active and more professional.

> **Examiner's tip**
>
> The reform of Parliament is an ongoing process. Examiners will be expecting candidates to have very up-to-date knowledge of the progress of reform.

Table 6.3 House of Lords reform proposals evaluated

Reform	Advantages	Disadvantages
Abolition	• It would save money. • It would streamline the legislative process. • It would remove obstructions from efficient government. • It would force the House of Commons to face up to its responsibilities.	• An important check on governmental power would be lost. • It would deny many worthy individuals the opportunity to engage in politics. • The expertise of the second chamber would be lost.
All appointed	• Many useful, knowledgeable individuals could be brought into politics. • It would be an opportunity to manipulate the membership to ensure a political and social balance. • It would be more independent than an elected chamber.	• It might put too much patronage power into the hands of the party leaders. • It would still be seen as undemocratic and lacking legitimacy.
Fully elected	• It is the most democratic solution. • Members would be fully accountable. • It would have more authority and so be a more effective check on governmental power. • If elected by proportional representation, it would reflect the strengths of the parties more accurately.	• It might become too influential and so obstruct the government excessively. • It might be unnecessary to have two elected chambers. • The people might be apathetic if faced by too many elections.
Mixed elected and appointed	• It would enjoy the advantages of both the main alternatives.	• It would suffer from the same problems as the two main alternatives.

Now test yourself

Tested ☐

4 For each of the following objectives, identify one proposed or achieved reform of either the Lords or Commons which has been designed to meet the objective:
(a) To increase the democratic legitimacy of the House of Lords
(b) To give backbench MPs more control of the parliamentary agenda
(c) To make constituency representation fairer
(d) To make MPs more accountable to their constituencies.

Answers on p. 108

Check your understanding

Tested ☐

1 Identify three functions of the House of Commons.
2 Identify three functions of the House of Lords.
3 Identify three limitations on the power of the House of Lords.
4 Identify three ways in which the whips seek to control MPs.
5 Give three ways that have been proposed to reform the House of Lords.
6 Identify three reforms of the House of Commons made by the coalition government of 2010.
7 Identify three ways in which Parliament can control governmental power.

Answers on p. 108

Exam practice answers and quick quizzes at **www.therevisionbutton.co.uk/myrevisionnotes**

Exam practice

Source questions

Read the passage and answer the questions that follow.

Despite the arrival of potentially weaker coalition government in 2010, the UK Parliament remains relatively powerless in the face of governmental power. The power of the party whips is based on prime ministerial patronage, party loyalty, collective responsibility and the constant threat that rebellious MPs will ultimately be dropped by their local party and so lose their seat. In the past, large government majorities have enabled the government to drive its legislation through, despite determined opposition. Departmental select committees and a more active House of Lords are rare examples of parliamentary power. The select committees cannot enforce their recommendations and the House of Lords' powers are limited by law. Even under coalition government, most legislative proposals are safe from parliamentary interference. New reforms now being proposed, however, suggest that the tide may be turning and that parliamentary power may increase in the future.

1 With reference to the source, outline two reasons why Parliament is dominated by the government. [5]

2 With reference to the source and your own knowledge, how can Parliament check the power of the government? [10]

3 How is it currently being proposed to strengthen Parliament in its control of the executive? [25]

Essay questions

4 Assess the various proposals for reform of the House of Lords. [40]

5 How effective is the House of Commons? [40]

6 Describe the role of parliamentary committees and assess their effectiveness. [40]

7 To what extent does the executive control Parliament? [40]

Answers and quick quiz 6 online

Online

Examiner's summary

✔ The UK Parliament has a number of functions. It is vital that students understand and can analyse all the main functions of both Houses of Parliament.

✔ The Houses of Lords and Commons have very distinct statuses and functions. Students should be able to describe these differences and analyse their significance.

✔ The relationship between Parliament and the government is the central feature of the British political system. Students must be able to describe and analyse the nature of this relationship, as well as being able to evaluate the power of the executive and the legislature.

✔ Knowledge of the work and status of parliamentary committees is important, including the main distinctions between different types of committee.

✔ Significant reform of Parliament began in 1997. Students should have full knowledge of reforms of both Houses. They should also be very up-to-date in their knowledge of reform.

✔ Reform of the House of Lords is a central issue. Students should be able to evaluate the different proposals for reform.

✔ Now that the issue of electoral reform is likely to be off the political agenda for the House of Commons, attention can shift to what kind of electoral system is being proposed for a possibly elected second chamber.

The relationship between the prime minister and the cabinet is a difficult one which requires a good deal of analysis. The arrival of coalition government has made the relationship even more complex. A key theme in British politics is an assessment of prime ministerial power, whether it continues to grow and whether it now amounts to presidentialism.

Role of the prime minister and cabinet

Nature of the cabinet
Revised

The cabinet in the UK has the following characteristics:

- It is composed of 20–25 senior politicians, all appointed directly by the prime minister.
- Members of the cabinet must be members of either the House of Commons (i.e. they are MPs) or the House of Lords (i.e. peers). If the prime minister wishes to appoint to cabinet someone who is neither an MP nor a peer, he or she must arrange for that person to be granted a life peerage so they can sit in the Lords.
- Normally one party wins an overall majority of the seats in the Commons and so forms a government alone. In this case *all* members of the cabinet will be from that governing party.
- Where — as in 2010 — there is a coalition, the members of cabinet can be from either of the parties in the coalition. In 2010, therefore, there were both Conservative and Liberal Democrat members of the cabinet.
- Cabinet normally meets once a week, but more often if there is a crisis or emergency, or if a special extra meeting is needed.
- The prime minister chairs the meetings (unless he or she is away for some reason, when their deputy takes over). Together with the **Cabinet Secretary,** the most senior civil servant, and therefore a neutral, non-elected official, the prime minister decides what will be discussed in the cabinet and notes in the **minutes** what was decided.
- A number of **cabinet committees** are created to deal in detail with specific areas of government policy. These have a small number of members (perhaps between 4 and 6) and are chaired by the prime minister or another senior cabinet member. Junior ministers, not in the cabinet, may also be members and they may invite interested and knowledgeable parties to advise them. Typical examples are Defence, Foreign Affairs, Environment, Education and Health.

> **Cabinet government** refers to the idea that the cabinet is the central decision-making body and lies at the heart of government. Many argue that it has been replaced by prime ministerial government.

> **Typical mistake**
>
> It is a serious mistake to believe that the cabinet is the main way in which government decisions and policies are developed. The cabinet does sometimes make policy, but it is usually merely legitimising decisions that have been made elsewhere.

- The minutes (detailed accounts) of the cabinet meetings remain a secret for at least 30 years. However, the main cabinet decisions are made widely known.
- Cabinet decisions are, effectively, official government policy.
- The prime minister has the power to dismiss ministers from the cabinet, to appoint new cabinet ministers, to create new cabinet posts or abolish old ones, and to move ministers around into different posts (known as a **reshuffle**).
- The cabinet works on the basis of **collective responsibility** (see below).

What is the role of the cabinet?   Revised ☐

The cabinet performs the following functions:

- It formalises and legitimises official government policy. Policies may have their origins elsewhere — for example, the prime minister, individual government departments, or the members of the governing party or parties — but they need the stamp of approval of the cabinet to become legitimate and generally recognised.
- It sometimes deals with disputes between different government departments and ministers when their proposals conflict or when there are problems allocating scarce government funds between different uses.
- It may meet in special session to deal with a crisis or emergency situation. There were, for example, a series of meetings to formulate a response to the banking and financial crisis that affected the UK in 2007–09. Dramatic events and large amounts of public expenditure were involved, so the cabinet had to discuss and approve the key decisions.
- Cabinet is where the presentation of policy is determined. This is to ensure that ministers co-ordinate the way in which policy is portrayed to the media and the public.
- The business of Parliament is arranged in the cabinet, in conjunction with the party whips. Ministers must be aware of what is happening in Parliament and when their presence is required.
- Policy formulation rarely takes place in cabinet, but from time to time the prime minister may invite the whole cabinet to discuss an important issue of the day. The decision to bid for the 2012 Olympics was certainly decided in cabinet, as has been the future of energy policy.

> **Core executive** is a name for the collective identity of central government. It comprises the prime minister, cabinet, other ministers, senior advisers and senior civil servants.

> **Examiner's tip**
>
> Examiners want to see critical awareness of the role of the cabinet. This should reflect the increasing marginalisation of the cabinet, but also an awareness of its remaining functions and importance.

What is the role of ministers?   Revised ☐

Government ministers have the following functions and status:

- They are senior members of the governing party or coalition.
- Most ministers have to manage a government department, being responsible for its policies and decisions.
- Ministers preside over the drafting of legislation and are responsible for managing proposed legislation through Parliament.

> **Political leadership** is a general term applying to all those who hold senior positions in government. It applies mostly to party leaders, ministers and other senior advisers.

- Ministers are assisted by large numbers of neutral civil servants and private advisers.
- The most senior ministers are appointed to the cabinet and thus become part of the central executive of the government.
- Cabinet ministers have a dual role — they manage their department and are part of the senior collective decision-making body.
- Ministers not in the cabinet are known as 'junior ministers'.

What is the prime minister?

The following are the main characteristics of the office of prime minister:

- The prime minister is the most senior minister in the government.
- The prime minister derives his or her authority from the monarch. Effectively the prime minister is the monarch's representative and so has all her powers. These powers, which have been transferred from monarch to prime minister, are known as **prerogative powers**.
- The prime minister is **head of government**, not **head of state**. However, he or she acts in place of the head of state (who is the queen) in most circumstances.
- The prime minister is the leader of the largest party in the House of Commons.
- The prime minister is not elected in any formal process; he or she is appointed automatically by the monarch as the leader of the largest party following an election.
- He or she is known as *primus inter pares*, a Latin phrase meaning 'first among equals'.
- *Primus inter pares* means that the prime minister is technically in the same position as any other minister, but it is acknowledged that he or she is the most senior of those ministers and therefore leads the government.

> **Prime ministerial government** is the idea that central government is now dominated by the prime minister to such a degree that the term 'prime ministerial' should be applied.

Now test yourself

1 Look at the following functions and tick the appropriate column to indicate whether they are normally the responsibility of the prime minister, the cabinet or individual ministers.

Function	Cabinet	Prime minister	Minister
Conducting foreign policy		✓	
Determining policy presentation	✓		
Appointing cabinet ministers		✓	
Managing government departments			✓
Settling disputes between ministers	✓		
Guiding legislation through Parliament			✓
Commander-in-chief		✓	
Debating major crises	✓		

Answers on p. 108

What is collective responsibility?

Collective responsibility is a key principle of British government. It maintains unity and underpins the importance of both the cabinet and the prime minister. The doctrine works like this:

- The cabinet is collectively responsible for all official government policy.
- All ministers must be prepared to defend official government policy, as legitimised by the cabinet.
- They must support government policy in public even if they disagree with it privately.
- Any minister who fails to support government policy must face dismissal.
- Ministers must resign if they intend to oppose government policy publicly.

Why is collective responsibility important?

Collective responsibility is important because:

- It maintains government unity.
- It helps the prime minister to maintain loyalty among his or colleagues.
- It prevents the opposition from dividing the government.

Table 7.1 shows examples of ministers who have resigned under the doctrine of collective responsibility.

Table 7.1 Resignations over collective responsibility

Minister and date	Issue
Robin Cook (Foreign Secretary), 2003 John Denham (Home Office minister), 2003	The decision to support the US-led invasion of Iraq
Clare Short (International Development Secretary), 2003	Post-Iraq war policies
James Purnell (Work and Pensions Secretary), 2009	General direction of policy under Gordon Brown's leadership
Lee Scott (junior ministerial aide), 2010 Mike Crockart (junior ministerial aide), 2010	The decision to allow universities to increase tuition fees

Collective responsibility is the principle that all government ministers are collectively responsible for all decisions of the government. It also means that ministers must publicly support all official policy or resign or face dismissal.

Typical mistake

Students often think that individual and collective responsibility are similar because they sound similar. However, there is a great difference between them and this should be reflected in examination answers.

Examiner's tip

When you discuss collective responsibility, the examiners expect to see not only how it operates with some examples from past resignations, but also why it is so important for the strength and working of central government.

What is individual ministerial responsibility?

Individual ministerial responsibility should not be confused with collective responsibility. It is important in defining the position of ministers. Its principles are as follows:

- A minister is responsible for all the decisions made by his or her department.
- The minister is responsible whether or not he or she was involved in the decision-making process.
- If the error is serious enough, the minister will be expected to resign or face dismissal, depending on whether he or she is supported by the prime minister.

Individual responsibility is the principle that each minister is responsible for the work of his or her department and must account for all its policies and decisions. Where serious errors are made, the minister may be required to resign. It also means that ministers may be obliged to resign for matters of personal misconduct.

● Ministers are also expected to resign over serious issues of personal misconduct.

Examples of resignations over individual responsibility are shown in Table 7.2.

Table 7.2 Resignations over individual responsibility

Minister and date	Reasons
Peter Mandelson (Northern Ireland Secretary), 1998	Embarrassing questions about a loan from another party member
Estelle Morris (Education Secretary), 2002	Her own admitted inability to deal with difficult education decisions
David Blunkett (Home Secretary), 2004	Questions about his department's role in possibly interfering with a visa application for a friend's nanny
Shahid Malik (Justice Minister), 2009	Questions about his expenses claims for housing (this was later overturned and he was reinstated)
Jacqui Smith (Home Secretary), 2010	Allegations that she had claimed expenses for videos hired by her husband
David Laws (Chief Secretary to the Treasury), 2010	Alleged financial irregularities

What has been the impact of coalition government?

Revised

In 2010 there was a hung parliament following the general election. This led to a coalition government between the Conservative Party and the Liberal Democrats. The impact of coalition has been as follows:

● The prime minister had to divide cabinet seats between the two coalition partners.

● He has to negotiate policy with his coalition partners.

● Collective responsibility comes under stress because the government is made up of two competing parties.

● Some policies cannot be agreed between the coalition partners and so result in 'agreements to differ'.

● The power of the prime minister has been reduced because he does not lead a completely united government.

● New appointments to cabinet from the small coalition partner have to be agreed with the leader of the coalition partner.

● The Liberal Democrat leader, Nick Clegg, became deputy prime minister.

> **Examiner's tip**
>
> Examiners will certainly be looking for analysis and illustration of how coalition government has affected the role, status and operation of the cabinet as well as its relationship with the prime minister.

Powers of the prime minister

What are the sources of prime ministerial power?

Revised

This question concerns the issue of from where the prime minister gains his or her authority to be head of government and to act in place of the head of state. In political systems that have a codified, supreme constitution, the source of power of the head of government is that constitution. In the UK there is no codified constitution, so the prime minister's power comes from other sources:

- Many of the prime minister's powers are **prerogative powers**. By convention, these are the monarch's powers that are delegated to the prime minister.
- The prime minister is head of the governing party. That party is another source of his or her power.
- The prime minister is also considered to be leader of the governing party in Parliament, so he or she derives authority from Parliament.
- The prime minister is head of the cabinet and so derives power from that body.
- We can also say that tradition is a source of power — the tradition that the leading cabinet minister is prime minister.

What are the powers of the prime minister?   Revised

The powers of the prime minister should be divided into two types, formal and informal.

- **Formal powers:** those that every prime minister has whatever the circumstances. These are prerogative powers that have been delegated from the monarch.
- **Informal powers:** these may vary according to the individual prime minister's circumstances.

Both types of power are shown in Table 7.3.

Table 7.3 Powers of the prime minister

Formal powers derived from being head of state and enjoying prerogative powers — these powers do not vary	Informal powers that vary according to the political circumstances of each prime minister — all holders of the office have them, but not in equal measure
<ul><li>To negotiate foreign treaties</li><li>To command the armed forces</li><li>To appoint or dismiss ministers</li><li>To determine the structure of government and the responsibilities of ministries</li><li>To be head of the civil service and determine its structure</li><li>To grant peerages and appoint people to important public posts</li></ul>	<ul><li>Chief policy-maker for the government</li><li>Represents the nation to foreign powers</li><li>Controls the business of the cabinet</li><li>Can make decisions that are required to deal with a short-term emergency situation</li></ul>

What are the limits to the prime minister's power?   Revised

Despite their considerable powers, prime ministers are subject to *important* limitations. These are the main ones:

- A prime minister must maintain the support of his or her party. If the party turns against the prime minister, he or she will lose a great deal of power and possibly lose office.

Examples: Margaret Thatcher (1979–90) lost the support of the Conservatives in 1989 over her support for the unpopular poll tax. She was voted out of office by her MPs. John Major (1990–97) lost support of a large minority of his party over European policy and his power was severely limited. Tony Blair (1997–2007) was forced to stand down as prime minister over continuing Labour opposition, mainly to the war in Iraq.

Examiner's tip

The examiners are often looking for a very critical examination of how powerful prime ministers really are. This means demonstrating a balance when explaining the strengths and weaknesses of the office. They are also looking for plenty of illustrations from the real experiences of past prime ministers to reinforce the analysis.

- A prime minister's strength depends on the size of his or her parliamentary majority. If it is small, the prime minister will have difficulty retaining the support of Parliament.

Example: John Major lost his large majority after the 1992 election and so lost authority.

- Prime ministers who lose the support of the media and the public will find their authority weakened.

Examples: Gordon Brown (2007–10) developed a weak image among the press and public.

- Events, often beyond his or her control, may weaken a prime minister.

Examples: Tony Blair lost much of his authority over the Iraq War and Gordon Brown suffered from the aftermath of the financial crisis of 2008–09.

- Occasionally the prime minister may be confronted by united cabinet opposition and will have to back down.

Example: Tony Blair hoped to bring Britain into the European single currency shortly after 1997, but most of the cabinet insisted the decision should be delayed.

- In a coalition government, the prime minister must take account of the views and demands of the coalition partners.

Example: David Cameron after 2010.

Now test yourself

Tested

2 Look at the following prime ministerial powers and tick the appropriate column to indicate whether they are enjoyed by all prime ministers, and are therefore permanent, or are variable.

Power	Permanent	Variable
Commander-in-chief	✓	
Policy making		✓
Patronage	✓	
Conducting foreign policy	✓	
Controlling the cabinet		✓

Answers on p. 109

Prime ministerial leadership

How does the prime minister control the cabinet?

Revised

It is acknowledged that prime ministers usually dominate their cabinets. This is achieved in a number of ways:

- The main device is patronage. The prime minister hires and fires ministers. This power means that most ministers are extremely loyal to the prime minister.

Exam practice answers and quick quizzes at **www.therevisionbutton.co.uk/myrevisionnotes**

- The prime minister controls the cabinet agenda and so is able to manipulate what policies are discussed.
- Prime ministers are known to use 'sofa politics'. This is when they have discussions with senior ministers *outside* cabinet (i.e. on the prime minister's office sofa), reach agreements and present the cabinet with a *fait accompli*.
- Prime ministers can manipulate the membership of important cabinet committees and so influence policy formulation.
- Prime ministers often use 'inner cabinets' of senior ministers to conduct government and so marginalise the cabinet. This often happens when a war is being conducted.
- In recent years, prime ministers have reduced drastically the length and frequency of cabinet meetings.

Appointment of cabinet ministers
Revised

What factors does a prime minister take into account when appointing cabinet ministers? There are two overall considerations:

1 Which individuals should be brought into the cabinet?

2 What should be the political 'balance' of the cabinet? In other words, the prime minister needs to create an effective team.

Individual considerations

These are qualities that an individual might have which makes him or her suitable for promotion to the cabinet. Here are some examples, illustrated from the cabinet of 2010–11:

- A close ally of the prime minister has an advantage, as he or she can be relied upon to support the leader (e.g. George Osborne).
- Promotion may be used as a reward for support in the past (e.g. Oliver Letwin).
- An individual may represent a significant section of the party, such as a right- or left-wing group (e.g. Theresa May).
- In a coalition government, key figures in the coalition partner's party must be included (e.g. Nick Clegg).
- A potential rebel may be included. Because of collective responsibility, such a potential opponent can be effectively silenced (e.g. Vince Cable).
- It may simply be that the prime minister foresees that an individual will be an effective minister, able to manage a department and implement policy successfully (e.g. Andrew Lansley).

Team considerations

Most prime ministers prefer a cabinet that is ideologically united and has no major political divisions.

- Some prime ministers select a *politically balanced* cabinet. This means that there will be members from different sections of the party. John Major, in the 1992–97 government, ensured that both the right wing and moderate sections of the party had representatives in the cabinet.

- In the case of the 2010 coalition, it was also necessary to balance the cabinet between the two parties in power. David Cameron chose 18 Conservatives and 5 Liberal Democrats.
- Prime ministers may also have one eye on *social balance*. So, for example, women or members of ethnic minorities may be represented for the sake of balance.

Prime ministerial power and its limitations are summarised in Table 7.4.

Table 7.4 Summary of prime ministerial power and its limitations

Power	Limitations
Prerogative power	Few limitations, although he or she could be overruled by the cabinet or Parliament.
Chief policy-maker	Could be overruled by his or her party, Parliament, the cabinet or a coalition partner. Could be overwhelmed by adverse events.
Parliamentary leader	Could lack a decisive majority following a general election. Could be overruled by a majority in Parliament.
Chief spokesperson for the government	Could develop a weak media or public image.

Increasing prime ministerial dominance

Revised

Modern UK government is often described as 'prime ministerial government', so dominant has the prime minister become. There are several reasons why the post of prime minister in the UK has become more dominant since the 1960s when the process began.

- Increasingly, the media have treated the prime minister as the single spokesperson of the government as a whole.
- Prime ministers have gradually exerted increasing control over their cabinets. The cabinet, in contrast, has become increasingly marginalised.
- The amount of advice available personally to the prime minister has steadily increased, with more special advisers, policy units and committees. This has led to a virtual 'Prime Minister's Department' located in Downing Street.
- Increasingly, prime ministers have learned to make policy through bilateral (one-to-one) arrangements with individual ministers.
- The patronage powers of the prime minister have been increasingly used to create loyalty.
- The increased use of collective responsibility (see below) has created more government loyalty.

Typical mistake

One of the main failings of candidates when answering questions about the prime minister is a lack of illustration from recent history. It is therefore very important to be able to illustrate analysis of the role and importance of the office by reference to the experience of at least two, and preferably three or four, prime ministers since Margaret Thatcher.

Is the prime minister now effectively a president?

Revised

Presidentialism is the theory that British prime ministers have effectively become presidents, even though they are not the head of state.

Exam practice answers and quick quizzes at **www.therevisionbutton.co.uk/myrevisionnotes**

Arguments in favour

So dominant has the prime minister become that some have argued that he or she is effectively a president. The reasons for this claim include the following:

- Prerogative powers are extremely important, especially as foreign relations and military matters have become more important than before the end of the Cold War. The prime minister's role as commander-in-chief and foreign policy leader makes him appear presidential.
- A theory known as **spatial leadership** has developed. This suggests that the prime minister is increasingly separated from the government and is seen as a lone figure, like a president.
- As explained above, there is effectively a 'Prime Minister's Department', which looks very like a president's establishment.
- The media increasingly treat the prime minister as if he or she were a president.

Arguments against

The following counter-arguments can be made:

- Prime ministers are not heads of state and so cannot claim to speak for the whole nation.
- There are important limitations on prime ministerial power that presidents do not face.
- The prime minister does not have a separate source of authority from the rest of the government, while presidents are responsible directly to the people.
- Some 'weaker' prime ministers certainly have not had a presidential image or style.

3 Look at the following features and tick the appropriate column to indicate whether they typically relate to a president or a prime minister or both.

Feature	Prime minister	President	Both
Responsible directly to the people		✓	
Elected separately from the government			
Can be removed from office by his or her party	✓		
Has powers of patronage			✓
Conducts foreign policy			✓
Accountable to the legislature	✓		
Is *primus inter pares*	✓		
Is head of state		✓	
Is commander-in-chief			✓

Answers on p. 109

Evidence of presidentialism from the experience of recent prime ministers, as well as counter-evidence, is shown in Table 7.5.

Table 7.5 Presidentialism and British prime ministers

Margaret Thatcher (1979–90)	**Positive** • She dominated the political system between 1982 and 1989. • She developed a dominant ideological position. • She led the mission to liberate the Falkland Islands in 1982. • She was admired abroad as a great spokeswoman for her country and her ideology. • She often claimed to represent Britain, notably in relations with Europe. **Negative** • She was ultimately removed by her party colleagues, not the people.
John Major (1990–97)	**Positive** • He led foreign policy in relation to Iraq. **Negative** • He was not a dominating personality and preferred to govern by consensus. • He had no strong ideological position. • He was limited by a divided, factional cabinet. • Without a comfortable parliamentary majority, his mandate was weak. • He had little international profile.
Tony Blair (1997–2007)	**Positive** • He led a new political movement – New Labour. • He built up a large policy-making machine reporting to him personally. • He committed the armed forces to four major actions – in Kosovo, Sierra Leone, Iraq and Afghanistan. • He became an important, well-respected world statesman. • He significantly weakened the cabinet and developed much policy personally. **Negative** • He was ultimately driven out of office by his party colleagues. • He lost his authority at home after the Iraq war.

(Continued)

Table 7.5 Presentialism and British prime ministers (*continued*)

Gordon Brown (2007–10)	**Positive**
	• He assumed a dominant personal leadership position during the financial crisis of 2007–09.
	• He was respected abroad for his handling of the financial crisis.
	Negative
	• His personal standing in the country began quite low and steadily declined.
	• He was limited by a divided cabinet.
	• He did not adopt a presidential 'style'.

Check your understanding

Tested

1 Outline three powers of a prime minister.
2 Outline three limitations on prime ministerial power.
3 Outline three roles of the cabinet.
4 Distinguish between collective and individual ministerial responsibility.
5 Outline three reasons why ministers resign.
6 What are the main differences between a head of government and a head of state?
7 Identify two examples of important ministerial resignations.
8 Identify three prerogative powers.

Answers on p. 109

Exam practice

Source questions

Read the passage and answer the questions that follow.

Possibly the most significant factor in the maintenance of stable government and prime ministerial power is the doctrine of collective responsibility. This principle requires that all ministers, whether in the cabinet or not, should defend government policy whether or not they disagree with it privately. Any minister who cannot do this must resign or face dismissal. Perhaps the most famous recent example of the doctrine at work occurred in 2003 when the Foreign Secretary, Robin Cook, resigned as he could not defend the UK's role in the Iraq war of that year. Collective responsibility is a way in which potential dissidents can be 'gagged'. It maintains government solidarity and prevents the opposition from finding ways to weaken the government's position. Furthermore, prime ministerial power is enhanced because the prime minister can use the doctrine to bring awkward ministers into line.

1 With reference to the source, outline two reasons why collective responsibility is important. [5]
2 With reference to the source and your own knowledge, how can a prime minister control his or her ministerial colleagues? [10]
3 Explain the main limits on the prime minister's control over the rest of the government. [25]

Essay questions

4 Is the prime minister now effectively a president? [40]
5 Do the limitations on the prime minister now outweigh his or her powers? [40]
6 Assess the current status and role of the cabinet. [40]
7 How has coalition government affected the role and functions of the prime minister and the cabinet? [40]

Answers and quick quiz 7 online

Online

Examiner's summary

✔ The relationship between the prime minister and the cabinet is a crucial one in British politics. It must be well understood and analysed.

✔ The prime minister has great powers but it is important to understand the limitations on those powers.

✔ It is important to understand the relationship between the prime minister, his or her party and Parliament.

✔ A key issue is the degree to which cabinet government has been in decline. The extent of and reasons for this decline need to be studied carefully.

✔ The prime minister's control over his or her cabinet must be understood, especially the importance of patronage.

✔ Illustrations from the experience of former prime ministers need to be used extensively.

✔ The principles of individual ministerial responsibility and collective responsibility are crucial and should be understood and evaluated.

✔ A key question concerns the extent to which the British prime minister has now become virtually a president.

✔ The impact of coalition government on the prime minister and the cabinet should be understood and analysed.

Exam practice answers and quick quizzes at **www.therevisionbutton.co.uk/myrevisionnotes**

8 Judges and civil liberties

Since the introduction of the Supreme Court especially, the status and importance of the senior judiciary has grown. Similarly the passage of the Human Rights Act has given the judiciary much greater ability to protect civil liberties. Since the 1990s a more active judiciary has come increasingly into conflict with government ministers. The judiciary has thus become a key element in the British system of government and politics.

Role of the judiciary

The term 'judiciary' is a collective name for judges and the courts over which they preside. We are here concerned with the upper levels of the judiciary who are involved in decisions of *political* importance.

The highest three levels of courts in the UK are these:

- the **High Court**, where important cases first appear
- the **Court of Appeal**, where appeals from lower courts are heard
- the **Supreme Court**, the highest court of appeal

In addition, cases involving Europe may be appealed higher to:

- the **European Court of Justice**, which deals with appeals on European Union law
- the **European Court of Human Rights**, which deals with appeals concerning the European Convention on Human Rights

> The **judiciary** is a collective name used to describe the judges in the UK. In terms of politics, the judiciary is the third branch of government, alongside the executive and the legislature. The political judiciary are involved in interpreting and applying law, asserting civil liberties and preventing public bodies from abusing their legal powers.

How do judges 'make law'?   Revised ☐

Judges make law in several ways:

- **Declaring common law.** A great deal of law is unwritten but is commonly believed to exist and to be enforceable. This is known as **common law**. Some common law — referring to the prime minister's powers or the status of individual rights, for example — has political importance. Where it is not clear what the common law is, judges may make a judgment on what the common law means and how it applies. Once a senior court has declared the meaning of common law, its interpretation is binding on all other lower courts.

- **Interpreting statute law.** Even laws drafted in government and passed by Parliament — **statutes** — may not be clear. In some appeals, the judges will declare what they believe the statute law means.

- **Developing case law.** Even if the wording of a statute is clear, it may not always be obvious how it should be applied in particular circumstances. Judgments of this kind are known as **case law** — law as applied to particular kinds of case. Once a piece of case law has been declared, it is binding on all lower courts when they consider very similar cases.

What kinds of case have political importance?

The following examples illustrate the political importance of the senior judiciary:

- They enforce the European Convention on Human Rights and other statutory or common law rights, whoever may have abused them.
- They interpret the meaning of human rights legislation.
- They enforce the 'rule of law', by which everyone is treated equally under the law, including government itself.
- They ensure that all sections of society are treated equally and prevent discrimination.
- They can prevent the government or any part of the state abusing or overstepping its statutory power.
- As explained above, they interpret law and so are part of the law-making process.
- Some of the judges' judgments may have an impact on important areas such as law and order, the welfare system, the health service, fair taxation and labour markets.

What is the independence of the judiciary?

How judicial independence works

- Judges cannot be dismissed on the basis of their decisions (they can be dismissed for misconduct such as bribery). This means that the government cannot put pressure on a judge by threatening him or her with dismissal. This is often described as **security of tenure**.
- The salaries of judges are protected and guaranteed. Again this prevents the government threatening a judge with loss of income if he or she will not co-operate.
- When a case is **sub judice**, meaning that it is under way in the courts, nobody, including the government and Parliament, is allowed to comment on it. This reduces political pressure on judges.
- Effectively, all judges are appointed by an independent Judicial Appointments Commission. This means that there is little or no political interference in appointments. In this way, judges do not owe any loyalty to politicians and can act independently.
- Senior judges are forbidden from engaging in active politics so that they have no party allegiances. Furthermore, as lifelong professional lawyers, they are used to putting aside their own personal views when making judgments.

> **Judicial independence** is the principle that the judiciary should be unaffected by politics. This means that judges should not be politically active and should be protected from any kind of political interference with their decision making.

Why judicial independence is important

- The rights of groups and individuals can be protected from abuse by government or other organisations.
- It is important that the government should not be allowed to exceed its legal powers.

Exam practice answers and quick quizzes at **www.therevisionbutton.co.uk/myrevisionnotes**

- The rule of law can be better protected by independent judges.
- When there is a need to interpret the meaning and operation of the constitution, it is important that the government is not able to manipulate the interpretation to suit itself.
- The judiciary should not be unduly influenced by any body or organisation in case it is required to dispense justice involving such a body.
- When there is a widespread public demand for certain draconian action to be taken — for example, discrimination against an ethnic minority, the violent suppression of dissident organisations or the torture of suspected terrorists — an independent judiciary can stand above public opinion and protect rights, equality and the rule of law.

What is judicial neutrality? — Revised

How judicial neutrality works

Judicial neutrality refers to characteristics of judges which should mean that their decisions are free from bias and prejudice. The main principles are as follows:

- Judges must not be politically active, and certainly must not be active members of a political party. Nor may they make any political statements.
- It is expected that judges should show no favour to any group in society: for example, on the basis of gender or ethnicity.
- As professional lawyers, judges are trained to make decisions based purely on law and on the rule of law, not on the basis of their own personal opinions.

Why is judicial neutrality important?

- It should ensure that judges treat all sections of the community equally and without prejudice.
- It prevents any political bias creeping into judgments.
- It gives confidence to citizens that they will be treated fairly.

Judicial neutrality is an aspiration that judges should be objective and not at all biased. Bias, or lack of it, affects various sections of society such as women and ethnic minorities. Judicial neutrality also means that judges are politically neutral, do not favour one political party over another and are not actively involved in political issues that might affect their judgment.

Typical mistake

Candidates often confuse judicial independence and judicial neutrality. They are not the same. Independence refers to the idea that the judiciary cannot be put under political pressure whereas neutrality refers to the desirability of an unbiased judiciary which will make fair judgments.

Now test yourself — Tested

1 Look at each of these features of the judiciary and decide whether they relate to **independence** or **neutrality**.

Feature	Independence	Neutrality
There should be a balance of men and women in the senior judiciary.		
The Supreme Court has been separated from Parliament.		
Many senior judges were educated privately.		
Judges may not be active members of a political party.		
Judges have security of tenure.		
The Judicial Appointments Commission appoints senior judges.		

Answers on p. 109

Power and influence of judges

What is judicial review?

How judicial review works

A judicial review is held in a senior court under a senior judge or judges in response to a request by an individual or association that wishes to challenge a decision or policy adopted by a public body, or a law passed by Parliament. The court reviews the decision on one of the following grounds:

- That it offends the European Convention on Human Rights (ECHR) — it is an abuse of civil liberties.

- That it offends a principle of common law.

- That it was *ultra vires* — that the body that made the decision did not have the legal power to do so. In other words, it was exceeding its legal powers.

- That it offended natural justice and/or the rule of law. This means that the individual or association did not receive equal treatment.

- That the correct administrative procedures were not followed in making a decision: for example, there was insufficient consultation.

The judgments of the courts in a judicial review are normally accepted as binding by government. However, if it is ruled that a piece of parliamentary legislation offends common law or the European Convention on Human Rights, the judgment may be ignored as Parliament remains sovereign.

Table 8.1 details some important examples of judicial reviews.

> **Typical mistake**
>
> Students sometimes confuse judicial reviews with legal appeal. An appeal is part of normal legal procedures, when a person may believe they have been wrongly convicted or have unjustly lost a case. These appeals are not normally of political significance. Judicial review concerns the actions of the government, a minister or any other public body and so is of political significance.

Table 8.1 Key examples of judicial reviews

Case	Effect
Mental Health Act case, 2002	The court ruled on the UK law that required that persons detained for mental health reasons had to prove their fitness for release. This offended the ECHR and so in future the authorities had to prove that a person was not fit to be released. The judgment asserted the human rights of those detained with mental illness.
Belmarsh case, 2004	The court ruled that persons detained as suspected terrorists could not be detained without trial as a result of the ECHR. It was a serious blow to the government's anti-terrorism policy.
Office of Fair Trading v. *Abbey National* (now Santander) *and others*, 2009	An *ultra vires* case in which the court ruled that the Office of Fair Trading had no legal power to investigate bank charging practices.
Suspected terrorist ban assets case, 2010	Court ruled that the government did not have the legal power to freeze the bank assets of suspected terrorists. An *ultra vires* case. The government later passed parliamentary legislation to allow it to freeze such assets.

> **Examiner's tip**
>
> Examples are perhaps more crucial in this topic than in any other. Students must use important cases of political significance to illustrate their writing. The exact details of the name of the case need not be quoted as long as it is clear what the case was about and why it was so important.

Exam practice answers and quick quizzes at **www.therevisionbutton.co.uk/myrevisionnotes**

Why is judicial review important?

> The **rule of law** is a constitutional and legal principle that all should be treated equally under the law and that the government itself must be subject to law and should not act outside the law.

The use of judicial review is important for these reasons:

- It helps to preserve the rule of law.
- It prevents government and the state abusing their powers.
- It ensures that no sections of the community are discriminated against.
- It makes public bodies accountable.
- It enforces the European Convention on Human Rights.

How can the judiciary control governmental power?

Revised

It is necessary to understand and evaluate the extent to which the judiciary controls the power of the government, the state in general and state agencies. It does this in a number of ways:

- By upholding the rule of law, it ensures that everyone is treated equally by government and other public bodies.
- By upholding civil liberties, the courts ensure that citizens' rights are not abused by government and state.
- The senior courts act as guardians over the powers exercised by government and public bodies. They do this by examining whether any body has exceeded the powers granted to it by law.
- The courts can adjudicate in a neutral and independent way if there is a dispute among government bodies, often between central government and regional or local bodies.
- The courts, including European courts, prevent the UK government or state from coming into conflict with European law, including the ECHR.

Now test yourself

Tested

2 Are the following facts about the judiciary true or false?

Fact	True	False
The Lord Chancellor is head of the judiciary.		
EU law is not binding on the UK Parliament.		
The European Court of Justice enforces the European Convention on Human Rights.		
Parliament can set minimum prison sentences for specific crimes.		
The Supreme Court can declare a UK law invalid if it conflicts with the ECHR.		

Answers on p. 110

Judicial and governmental power

Examiner's tip

Examiners like to see good evaluations of the power of the judiciary. This means well-balanced analyses, demonstrating both the strengths and the weaknesses of the judiciary in its roles of protecting rights and controlling abuses of government.

So how effectively can the judiciary control governmental power?
Table 8.2 presents an evaluation of judicial power over government.

Table 8.2 Evaluation of judicial power over government

Strengths	Weaknesses
• Judicial reviews have a wide scope to deal with claimed abuses of governmental power. • The Human Rights Act has given judges added power to prevent government from exercising excessive powers that threaten people's rights. • The conventions and statutes concerning the independence of the judiciary have resulted in a more active judiciary. • Judges retain wide powers over the sentencing of convicted criminals.	• The absence of a codified constitution and the existence of ill-defined government powers make it difficult to judge whether power has been abused. • Parliamentary sovereignty means that a government that controls a parliamentary majority can grant powers to itself or its agencies through legislation and the judiciary can do nothing to prevent this. • Parliament can place constraints on the judiciary in its sentencing powers. • Government and Parliament can claim that judges are unelected and unaccountable, and so do not have the right to challenge the power of the elected and accountable government and Parliament.

Judicial power in practice

A number of recent cases (all from 2010) illustrate the power of the courts in relation to government:

- *Child Poverty Action Group* v. *Secretary of State for Work and Pensions.* This *ultra vires* case made an important ruling that the Department of Work and Pensions did not have the legal power to force people to return overpayments of welfare benefits when the Department was at fault.

- *Family of Justin Smith* v. *Secretary of State for Defence.* The court ruled that the European Convention on Human Rights does *not* normally have any force with troops serving abroad.

- *H. M. Treasury* v. *Mohammed Jabar Ahmed.* The court ruled that the government did *not* have the power to freeze the financial assets of suspected terrorists.

Examiner's tip

It is always advantageous, though not absolutely necessary, to be as up to date as possible. This particularly means knowing about recent cases of political significance.

Civil liberties and individual rights

What are civil liberties?

Civil liberties are the freedoms and rights that all citizens have, or believe they have, which are guaranteed by law and the state. Most civil liberties are contained today in the European Convention on Human Rights (ECHR). The ECHR was brought into British law by the Human Rights Act of 1998.

Civil liberties are a name given to the freedoms ands rights which are, or might be, protected by the state and the law.

What is the Human Rights Act?

The Human Rights Act (HRA) was passed in 1998 and came into force in 2000. Its effect was to bring the terms of the European Convention on Human Rights into British law. The following arrangements were made under the Act:

- All government bodies, state organisations, devolved assemblies and governments, local authorities and any body engaged in 'public business', such as schools, hospitals and the media, must abide by its terms.

- The only body that is not bound by the convention is the UK Parliament in Westminster. This means that parliamentary sovereignty is preserved.

- If legislation is proposed in Westminster which is likely to contradict the convention, the relevant government minister must make a 'declaration of incompatibility', stating how and why the proposal does not conform to the convention.

- Any legal claim that the convention has been breached can be made in a British court at any level. If the judge believes the convention has been breached, he or she can order that a decision or action must be changed or cancelled.

- Appeals based on the convention can be passed up to higher courts, ultimately to the Supreme Court.

- Judges in the courts can interpret the meaning of the convention and how it should apply in a particular case.

- The one limitation on the power of the judges is that they cannot set aside any law made in the UK Parliament. The judge may declare that the convention has been breached by such an Act or order, but he or she cannot overturn it.

- In some cases of great significance, a final appeal may be made to the European Court of Human Rights in Strasbourg.

- Judgments of the European Court are binding in most countries, but not in the UK. Nevertheless the UK government will virtually always abide by the decisions of the European Court.

Examples of terms of the European Convention on Human Rights

A wide range of rights are asserted in the ECHR. Some examples of prominent rights are:

- the right to life
- the right to privacy and family life
- the right to free expression
- the right to free assembly
- the right to free belief
- the right to be free from discrimination of various kinds
- the right to a fair trial

Table 8.3 shows three important cases brought under the ECHR.

Table 8.3 European Convention on Human Rights cases

Case	Detail
Afghan hijackers case, 2006	A controversial ruling that a group of Afghan refugees who had hijacked a plane to the UK could claim asylum and seek work in the UK on the grounds that their lives would be in danger if they were deported.
Mosley v. *News of the World*, 2008	Max Mosley, a Formula 1 executive, claimed that his privacy had been invaded when details of a sadomasochist party he attended were reported in the *News of the World*, with several false details. He was awarded compensation.
Insurance discrimination case, 2011	The European Court of Human Rights ruled that insurance companies could not discriminate against men by charging them higher car insurance premiums than women.

Now test yourself

Tested

3 Consider the following situations and decide which civil liberty or liberties are involved.
   (a) The courts can issue super-injunctions that prevent publication of private matters in the media and keep the name of the person concerned a secret.
   (b) The police may decide to ban a demonstration on the grounds of public order.
   (c) Government could declare membership of a political party illegal on the grounds that the party threatens the state.
   (d) Taking away the passports of well-known football hooligans before the World Cup.

Answers on p. 110

How do the courts uphold civil liberties?

Revised

There are several ways in which judges in the UK and in the European Court of Human Rights and European Court of Justice (see p. 99) can protect individual and group rights:

- They can refer to the European Court of Human Rights and decide that a right has been infringed. They may reverse a decision and/or order compensation.
- They may declare that common law has been breached and change a decision.
- They may refer to a parliamentary statute (such as equal opportunities legislation) which protects a particular right. This will be enforced.
- They may similarly refer to a piece of European Union legislation.
- A judicial review may take place at the request of a citizen.

How well can the courts uphold civil liberties?

Revised

The courts have strengths and weaknesses in seeking to uphold civil liberties.

Strengths

- The passage of the Human Rights Act has added a codified set of rights to which judges can refer.

Exam practice answers and quick quizzes at **www.therevisionbutton.co.uk/myrevisionnotes**

- Particularly since the 1960s, a large quantity of legislation has been passed that asserts civil liberties, particularly laws forbidding discrimination of various kinds.
- As the judiciary has become steadily more independent, it has also become more active in its protection of rights.
- The growth of judicial review, to encompass many thousands of cases each year today, has brought judges to the forefront of enforcing rights and equality.

Limitations

- The courts cannot be proactive in their protection of rights. This means they must wait for appeals to be launched by citizens.
- Because the European Convention on Human Rights is not binding on Parliament, the judges are powerless to overturn laws that infringe rights.
- When judges do assert rights through common law or the ECHR, they cannot prevent the government from passing new legislation to prevent the courts making similar decisions in the future.

The role of European courts

Revised ☐

Two courts are relevant here.

European Court of Human Rights

The European Court of Human Rights (ECHR) sits in Strasbourg (France) and hears appeals from citizens from all parts of Europe. It bases its decisions on the European Convention on Human Rights, to which most European countries are signatories. *This court is not part of the European Union.*

European Court of Justice

Based in Luxembourg, the European Court of Justice (ECJ) is the highest court of the European Union. It has a number of roles:

- It settles legal disputes between EU member states.
- It settles disputes between the European Commission and a member state.
- It interprets the meaning of EU law and decides how it should be applied in specific cases and to individual countries.
- It hears appeals from individuals and groups who feel that their economic or social rights under EU law may have been abused within their own country.
- The judgments of the ECJ are binding on all member states including the UK.

Typical mistake

It is common for students to confuse the roles of the European Court of Justice and the European Court of Human Rights. This can cause problems. The European Court of Justice is the highest court of appeal in the European Union. The European Court of Human Rights, by contrast, has nothing to do with the European Union. It is the court that hears appeals concerning the European Convention on Human Rights, which is not administered by the EU.

Table 8.4 Key European cases

ECHR cases	Detail
Votes for prisoners, 2005	Court ruled that the UK's denial of prisoners' right to vote was an abuse of their rights. In 2011 Parliament voted to ignore this ruling.
DNA retention case, 2008	Court ruled that it was against the ECHR right to privacy to retain the DNA profile of persons who have not been convicted of a crime. The government was forced to destroy many DNA profiles.
Stop and search powers, 2010	Court ruled that it was an abuse of rights for the police to stop and search attenders at demonstrations without any cause. These powers are now under review.
ECJ cases	**Detail**
Factortame case, 1991	A landmark ruling that stated that the laws of the UK (in this case, the Merchant Shipping Act) could not conflict with EU law (in this case, the common fisheries policy). Effectively this transferred much sovereignty to EU law.
Jobseeker's allowance, 2004	Court ruled that citizens of any EU state could claim jobseeker's allowance in the UK.
Retirement age, 2009	Court ruled in favour of the UK's right to introduce a compulsory retirement age at 65.
Car insurance, 2011	Court ruled that it was against EU law for car insurance companies to charge a different premium to men and women. Insurance companies have to change their charges.

Reform of the judiciary

Revised ☐

The main recent reforms of the judiciary were contained in the Constitutional Reform Act of 2005. Is main provisions were these:

● The Lord Chancellor, who had been head of the legal system, a cabinet minister and Speaker of the House of Lords, was to lose most of his roles and return to a largely ceremonial position.

● The Lord Chief Justice — a non-political judge — was put in charge of the legal system.

● A new political post of Secretary of State for Justice was created. The holder sits in cabinet, but is forbidden from interfering with court decisions.

● A new Supreme Court was set up (it began operation in 2009). This has the same powers as the Judicial Committee of the House of Lords (known as the 'Law Lords'), which it replaced. It is the highest appeal court in the UK and is now separate from the House of Lords. New members of the court will not necessarily be granted a peerage.

● Appointments to the Supreme Court were to be made by a senior judicial committee which is free from political interference.

Typical mistake

It is a common mistake among students to believe that the Supreme Court has the power to overturn a parliamentary statute. This is wrong. The court can express an *opinion* that a law is unjust, but it cannot overturn or amend it. This is because Parliament is sovereign. Judges can also *interpret* laws in their own way, but not actually overturn them.

- Appointments to the judiciary in general were put in the hands of an independent Judicial Appointments Commission. Again this is free from political interference, although the prime minister can veto a controversial appointment.

Main effects of constitutional reform

Revised

The main effects of constitutional reform as regards the judiciary were as follows:

- It is generally agreed that the judiciary was made more independent.
- The independent status of the judiciary meant that it felt more confident about exercising its powers.
- Increased judicial activism means that judges have become more willing to challenge governmental power and to assert civil liberties.
- The improved legitimacy of the judiciary has encouraged judges to be more outspoken on legal, constitutional and political issues.
- It has brought the judiciary increasingly into conflict with governments.

Examples of judiciary–government conflict

- Judges assert their right to make decisions on sentencing of convicted criminals while governments have insisted that this is a political issue to be determined by them, as they are elected and accountable while judges are unelected and unaccountable.
- Judges have been active in protecting civil liberties. However, governments have a responsibility to protect the security of the state. Sometimes the security of the state and maintaining civil liberties (for example, of suspected terrorists) come into conflict.
- In 2011 conflict erupted over the issues of privacy and freedom of the press. On the whole judges preferred to safeguard personal privacy against press and media intrusion. Government, on the other hand, was determined to protect freedom of the media.
- In general, ministers have become uneasy about an increasingly active and independent judiciary interpreting law instead of leaving Parliament to do this.

> **Examiner's tip**
>
> Many questions require an overall assessment of the status of the judiciary. This means being able to analyse and apply the fact that judges are unelected and unaccountable. Examiners hope to see candidates demonstrate their understanding that politicians feel better placed to pronounce on how the law works because they are elected and accountable, and should reflect public opinion.

Check your understanding

Tested

1 Identify three civil liberties.
2 Outline two reasons for judicial review.
3 Distinguish between the European Court of Justice and the European Court of Human Rights.
4 Describe any two important human rights cases.
5 Outline three ways in which judges 'make law'.
6 Outline three ways in which judicial independence is maintained.
7 Outline three aspects of judicial neutrality.

Answers on p. 110

Exam practice

Source questions

Read the passage and answer the questions that follow.

The new Supreme Court, which began work in 2009, has marked a major landmark in judicial activism and independence. The UK's most senior judges were effectively removed from the House of Lords and so were more able to express their independence from the rest of the political system. Although the new court has not been given any additional powers, it has used its independence to be more active both in the protection of civil liberties and in preventing government from exercising excessive, unjustified power. The process of judicial review has expanded enormously and enabled judges to enforce the rule of law more robustly. Governments have responded by complaining that judges have too much power. In particular, they say that unelected, unaccountable judges should not be allowed to thwart the plans of elected ministers. To make the problem more serious, judges are behaving more independently, especially since the method of appointing them was taken out of political hands in 2005.

1 With reference to the source, explain two roles of the Supreme Court. [5]

2 With reference to the source and your own knowledge, explain how the independence of the judiciary is maintained. [10]

3 How and why have senior judges come into conflict with government ministers since 1997? [25]

Essay questions

4 Are judges now too politically powerful? [40]

5 Why and how have judges come into conflict with government? [40]

6 How effectively can and do judges protect civil liberties? [40]

7 How effectively can and do judges control governmental power? [40]

Answers and quick quiz 8 online

Online

Examiner's summary

✔ Judges are involved in making law after it has developed over time or been passed by Parliament. Examiners may ask about this process and will expect you to know why judges' role in law making can have political significance.

✔ The roles of senior courts in the UK and Europe must be understood, but especially why these roles affect political outcomes and processes.

✔ Examiners will expect candidates to be able to demonstrate knowledge and understanding of how the judiciary has been reformed, particularly how its powers have been enhanced by judicial review and the Human Rights Act, and how its independence has been improved.

✔ In the case of all answers, examiners expect candidates to include appropriate examples in the form of important political cases.

✔ Examiners will seek evidence that candidates understand why the independence and neutrality of the senior judiciary is important.

✔ The issue of whether judges should have the power to resolve political issues through legal judgments must be addressed. The contrast between unelected, unaccountable judges, who are nevertheless independent and neutral, and politicians who are subject to public opinion should be understood and evaluated.

Answers

Chapter 1

Now test yourself

1

Institution	How the institutions can be said to be representative
MPs	MPs represent the interest of their constituency and of constituents. They tend to represent their party's policies. They may see themselves as representing the public interest. Some MPs represent sectional or promotional pressure groups.
House of Commons	The House exists to represent the national interest in case it conflicts with government policy. It is also the guardian of the government's mandate on behalf of the people. The House may represent the interests of minorities against the majority government.
House of Lords	The Lords tends to represent minorities, and sectional and promotional groups. It also safeguards the national interest in case there is a conflict with the will of the Commons.
Political parties	Most British parties claim they represent the national interest. Parties may also single out sections of the community that they particularly represent, such as the working class, the poor or minorities.
Pressure groups	Nationalist parties represent the UK's national minorities. Pressure groups represent sections of the community, such as occupational groups or groups that seek to promote a specific cause.

2

Why the referendum was necessary	Example(s) of such a referendum	Outcome
To achieve popular consent to a constitutional change.	On devolution to Scotland in 1997	A large majority in favour of devolution
The government itself was divided on the issue.	The vote on the introduction of the alternative vote in 2011. The coalition partners disagreed on this issue.	A large majority rejected AV
It was necessary to achieve widespread consent for a specific reason.	The 1998 referendum to approve the Good Friday Agreement, designed to bring peace and power sharing to Northern Ireland	A resounding 'Yes' vote on a large turnout
To entrench an important constitutional change, preventing it from being overturned by a future parliament.	All the devolution referendums in 1997	All resulted in a 'Yes' vote

3 (a) The proposal to allow constituents to recall MPs and force a by-election if an MP proves to be unsatisfactory in his or her conduct. This would empower people and remove poor MPs.

(b) Possibly introduce votes at 16 to accustom young people to becoming involved. The coalition proposal for regular petitions and more referendums would include more people in political processes.

(c) Maintain and extend citizenship education as a way of informing young people about politics.

(d) Possibly introduce proportional representation to eliminate wasted votes and make votes of equal value. Possibly make it easier for people to vote by weekend elections or internet voting.

Check your understanding

1 Direct democracy is a form of democracy and description of political decision making where the people affected make the decisions themselves or have a direct input into decision making. The most common device used is the referendum. It contrasts with representative democracy.

2 Representative democracy is a common form of democracy where the people elect representatives who make decisions on behalf of the people. Representative democracies typically use members of a parliament, parties and pressure groups to represent the people.

3 Look at the definitions above and pick out the key distinctions, such as elections versus referendums and the difference in who makes decisions.

4 A referendum is a vote by which the people make an important decision themselves rather than leaving the decision to elected representatives. It is always in response to a question with a simple yes/no answer. Referendums are usually held to determine important decisions concerning government or taxation. Referendums may be national, regional or local. They are a pure form of democracy.

5 Examples of referendums include:
- the vote to decide whether the UK would remain in the EU in 1975
- votes to approve devolution to Scotland and Wales in 1997
- the vote to decide whether to use the alternative vote for general elections

There are other examples of regional and local referendums.

6 People can participate in politics in any of the following ways:
- voting in elections
- joining political parties
- actively engaging in political campaigns
- joining a pressure group
- standing for electoral office

7 Liberal democracy is a form of representative democracy where there is strong protection for rights and freedoms, where the rule of law prevails, government is subject to strong constitutional controls and there is widespread tolerance of political ideas and movements.

Chapter 2

Now test yourself

1 Three main functions are:

(a) Developing policies and political programmes. This provides choices for the electorate and educates the electorate about political issues.

(b) Recruiting candidates and leaders. This ensures good-quality representatives.

(c) Educating the public about political issues. A well-informed electorate enhances democracy.

2

Idea	Left-wing idea	Right-wing idea
1 The redistribution of real income from rich to poor through tax policies	✓	
2 The bringing of major industries under state control	✓	
3 A belief in free markets and low taxation		✓
4 Opposition to strong trade unions		✓
5 Strong support for the welfare state	✓	
6 A hard line on crime, law and order		✓

3

Ideas/policies	New Right	Traditional
1 A belief in the organic society		✓
2 Support for traditional institutions		✓
3 Curbing trade union power	✓	
4 A pragmatic approach to policy making		✓
5 Non-interference by government in economic management	✓	

4

Policy or idea	New Labour	Traditional Labour
1 A belief in strong trade unions		✓
2 Low corporate taxation	✓	
3 Regulation of free market capitalism	✓	
4 Very progressive tax to redistribute income		✓
5 Stress on individualism rather than collectivism	✓	

Check your understanding

1 A political party is an association of people with similar political views who come together with the purpose of securing election to political bodies and usually of forming a government or sharing in governmental power.

2 Any three of the following functions:
- developing policies and political programmes
- educating the public on political issues
- representing sections of the population
- recruiting and training political leaders
- running election campaigns

3 Any two of the following Conservative policies:
- the long-term reduction of taxation
- restoring responsibility in public finances
- reform of the NHS to make it more responsive to demands
- reforming education to provide more parental choice
- stronger measures to deal with crime levels
- reforming welfare to prevent fraud and target it more effectively

4 Any two of the following Labour policies:
- increasing social mobility
- poverty reduction
- protection of welfare services including health and education
- redistributing some income from rich to poor
- improving environmental protection
- targeting welfare benefits more effectively

5 Any two of the following Liberal Democrat policies:
- stronger protection of human rights
- strong environmental protection measures
- reform of the constitution
- redistribution of income from rich to poor
- strong protection for women and minority groups
- introduction of a fairer taxation system
- a less interventionist foreign policy

6 Any two of the following policies that enjoy a wide consensus of support:
- better targeting of welfare benefits
- retention of the principles of the welfare state
- reform of the House of Lords

- stricter rules on harmful emissions
- reform of the banking sector

7 Any two of the following policies that are subject to adversary politics:

- how quickly the government needs to reduce its budget deficit
- the further use of nuclear energy as against renewable sources
- how closely integrated with the European Union the UK should be
- how to deal with crime issues — whether to use harsher or more liberal remedies for crime
- the extent to which the burden of taxation should fall mainly on the better off in society

3

Feature	Electoral system
Voters choose a party rather than a candidate	Regional list
Voters are given the widest choice of candidates	Single transferable vote
Produces the most proportional result	Regional list
Preserves the strongest MP–constituency link	First-past-the-post
Is often used to elect a single office-holder	Supplementary vote
Voters can vote both for a candidate and for a party	Additional member system

Chapter 3

Now test yourself

1

Positives	Negatives
They tend to produce a clear winner.	Governments are elected on a minority of the popular vote.
They give the electorate a clear choice.	They discriminate against small parties.
They are simple to understand.	Too many votes are wasted.
There is a strong MP–constituency relationship.	MPs are often elected on a minority vote.

2

Political system	Electoral system	Features, party system and typical type of government
Scottish Parliament	Additional member system	- Some candidates stand in constituencies; others are on regional party lists. - Result tends to be proportional. - Small parties can gain seats. - There is a four-party system. - Coalition or minority government normally (SNP majority in 2011).
Northern Ireland Assembly	Single transferable vote	- Wide voter choice. - A five-party system with no dominant party. - Multi-seat constituencies. - Proportional result. - Power-sharing government.
London Mayor election	Supplementary vote	- The winner has an overall majority. - Voters have two choices.
European Parliament	Regional list	- Produces a very proportional result. - Voters choose parties, not individual candidates.

Check your understanding

1 First-past-the-post is the electoral system used for general elections in the UK. The key elements are: the country is divided into constituencies, each of which returns one MP. Voters have one vote each. The winner in each constituency is the candidate who achieves the most votes, not necessarily an overall majority of the votes. The government is formed by the party or coalition of parties that has an overall majority of the seats in the House of Commons.

2 The key elements of STV are: There are multi-member constituencies. In Northern Ireland each constituency returns six representatives. Voters place candidates in their order of preference. They may vote for as many or few of the candidates as they wish. An electoral quota is calculated on a special formula. This is the total votes divided by the number of seats plus 1, a further one being added to the resultant number. Any candidate who achieves this quota on first preference votes is elected. Thereafter, the lower preference 'spare' votes of the elected candidates are redistributed. When six candidates have achieved the quota after the redistribution of spare votes, they are elected. The outcome is roughly proportional to the seats cast for each party.

3 AMS is the system used for devolved elections in Scotland, Wales and the Greater London Assembly. About two-thirds of the seats are elected on the first-past-the-post system. The rest of the seats are awarded through a regional list system. Voters have two votes each, one for a constituency member and the other for a party. These regional list seats are awarded in proportion to the votes cast for each party, with some adjustment to make the outcome as proportional as possible.

4 In the regional list system, the country is divided into regions. In each region parties offer a list of candidates. Voters vote for one of the party lists, not for individual candidates. Seats are awarded to each party in each region, in proportion to the number of votes cast for the party within that region. The outcome is very proportional to support for each party.

5 SV is used to elect a single individual to office, for example the London mayor. Each voter has two votes, a first and second choice. If a candidate achieves over 50% of first-choice votes, he or she is elected. If no one does, all the candidates drop out except for the top two. The second preference votes for these top two are then added to their first choices. The winner is the one who wins this second round of votes.

6 Any three of the following impacts:

- One party usually wins an overall majority in the House of Commons (though this did not occur in 2010).
- The larger parties tend to win a disproportionately large share of the seats available.
- Smaller parties win less than a proportional share of the seats.
- Very small parties tend to win no seats at all.
- Many MPs are elected without achieving an overall majority of seats in their constituency.
- It favours parties with geographically concentrated support.

7 Proportional representation describes a political system and especially its electoral system which tends to award representative seats in a parliament or assembly in general proportion to the votes cast for each party. STV, AMS and regional list systems are examples of proportional representation electoral systems.

Chapter 4

Now test yourself

1 (a)

Group	Sectional	Promotional
National Union of Mineworkers	✓	
Amnesty International		✓
National Trust		✓
Taxpayers' Alliance	✓	
Campaign for Real Ale	✓	✓

(b)

Group	Insider	Outsider
Greenpeace		✓
National Farmers' Union	✓	
RSPCA	✓	
Countryside Alliance		✓

2

Method	Examples
Civil disobedience	Greenpeace, Animal Liberation Front
Sitting on policy advisory committees	National Farmers' Union, Confederation of British Industry
Lobbying the European Union	Most trade unions, fishing industry
Organising public demonstrations	UK Uncut, Friends of the Earth

3

Activity	Enhance democracy	Threaten democracy
Campaigns of civil disobedience		✓
Mass membership	✓	
Use of large amounts of finance		✓
Insider links with government		✓

Check your understanding

1 Any three of the following functions:
- acting as a channel of communication between citizens and the state
- educating the public on political issues
- protecting minorities
- informing government of issues and opinions
- dispersing power and so improving democracy

2 Any promotional pressure groups can be chosen, but some prominent examples are: Liberty, Friends of the Earth, Greenpeace, ASH, UK Uncut.

3 Any sectional pressure groups can be chosen, but some prominent examples are: National Farmers' Union, Taxpayers' Alliance, Confederation of British Industry, British Medical Association, Automobile Association.

4 Any insider pressure groups can be chosen, but prominent examples are: National Farmers' Union, Institute of Directors, Royal College of Nursing, Age UK.

5 Any outsider pressure groups can be chosen but prominent examples are: Greenpeace, Plane Stupid, Countryside Alliance, UK Uncut.

6 Examples of direct action are: public demonstrations, acts of civil disobedience, media campaigns, internet campaigns, publicity stunts.

7 Any three of these reasons:
- financial power
- large membership
- insider status
- involvement of celebrities
- wide agreement with the policies of the current government
- high degree of organisation
- holding a strategic position in society, such as doctors or teachers

8 Any three of these reasons:
- may be powerful countervailing (opposing) pressure groups
- may not enjoy the sympathy of government
- alienation of public support
- lack of finance
- small membership and low profile

Chapter 5

Now test yourself

1

Characteristic	Codified	Uncodified
It is not very flexible.	✓	
It is a strong safeguard of rights.	✓	
It can adapt to changing circumstances.		✓
It has a number of different sources.		✓
It can be easily interpreted by judges.	✓	
It can be found in one single document.	✓	
It is likely to be entrenched.	✓	

2

Source	Example
Constitutional conventions	Salisbury Convention preventing the House of Lords obstructing government mandate measures, collective cabinet responsibility
Books of constitutional authority	Dicey's *Constitutional Laws*, Bagehot's *English Constitution*
Constitutional statutes	Human Rights Act, Scotland and Wales Acts
EU treaties	Maastricht Treaty, Lisbon Treaty

3 (a) Scottish Parliament

(b) General election

(c) European Union

(d) Government

(e) Referendum

4 (a) Human Rights Act

(b) Devolution

(c) House of Lords reform

(d) Fixed-term parliaments

(e) Supreme Court

(f) Freedom of Information Act

(g) Introducing proportional representation

(h) Introducing equal-sized constituencies

Check your understanding

1 Any three of the following sources:

- parliamentary statutes
- conventions
- EU treaties
- common law
- books of constitutional authority
- traditions

2 Any three of the following functions:

- distributing power among political institutions
- establishing political processes and relationships
- establishing the limits to governmental power
- safeguarding the rights of citizens
- establishing rules of citizenship and nationality
- establishing procedures for the amendment of the constitution itself

3 Any three of the following features:

- constitutional monarchy
- unitary
- a bias towards executive power
- the rule of law
- not codified and therefore flexible
- based on parliamentary sovereignty

4 Any three of the following constitutional reforms:

- devolution
- Human Rights Act
- Lords reform
- Freedom of Information Act
- introduction of the Supreme Court
- elected mayors
- London government

5 Any three of the following constitutional reforms:

- fixed-term parliaments
- election by MPs of select committee chairs
- backbench business committee established
- recall of MPs by dissatisfied constituents
- reduction in the size of the House of Commons
- increased powers to the Welsh Assembly

6 Unitary constitutions are those where legal sovereignty resides in one, central location. In the case of the UK, sovereignty lies with the Westminster Parliament. Power may be devolved, but it can be restored to the central, sovereign authority.

7 A federal constitution, such as that of the USA, is one where sovereignty is distributed between central authorities and regional bodies. This distribution of sovereignty is established within a codified and entrenched constitution.

Chapter 6

Now test yourself

1 (a) The Commons is elected; the Lords is not.

(b) The Commons can veto legislation; the Lords can only delay it.

(c) MPs represent constituencies; Peers do not.

(d) Government has a majority in the Commons but not in the Lords.

(e) The Commons scrutinises the government's financial affairs; the Lords has no such power.

2 Reasons for government domination:

- It normally enjoys an overall majority of MPs.
- MPs tend to be loyal to their party.
- The influence of prime ministerial patronage.

Ways in which Parliament can control government:

- It can veto legislation.
- Departmental select committees investigate government activities robustly.
- The Commons can dismiss a government with a vote of no confidence.

3

Feature	Help government?	Help Parliament?
There is strong party loyalty	✓	
MPs have strong constituency links		✓
Votes of no confidence		✓
Departmental select committees		✓
MPs' research capability	✓	
Party whips	✓	
The Parliament Act 1949	✓	
Legislative committees in the Commons	✓	
Legislative committees in the Lords		✓
Crossbenchers in the Lords		✓
Political patronage	✓	

4 (a) An elected second chamber

(b) Backbench business committee

(c) Equal-sized constituencies

(d) Power of constituency recall

Check your understanding

1 Any three of the following functions of the House of Commons:

- scrutinising legislation
- giving formal consent and legitimacy to legislation
- checking abuses of power by government
- representing the interests of constituencies and regions
- representing the interests of minorities
- ensuring government is efficient and democratic
- forcing ministers to be accountable for their actions

2 Any three of the following functions of the House of Lords:

- amending legislation in order to improve it
- delaying legislation, forcing government to rethink proposals
- deliberating on the great issues of the day
- protecting the interests of minorities

3 Any three of the following limitations:

- It can only delay legislation for 1 year.
- Its proposed amendments must be approved by the Commons.
- The Salisbury Convention prevents it obstructing government proposals that were in its election manifesto.
- It has no power over financial matters.

4 Any three of the following ways:

- appealing to their sense of party loyalty
- reminding them that rebelliousness might threaten their career ambitions
- doing deals to secure their compliance, such as offering decisions favourable to their constituencies
- threatening to have them de-selected by their local party and so lose their candidacy at the next election

5 Any three of the following proposals:

- complete abolition
- to be fully elected by proportional representation
- to be partially elected, partially appointed
- to be fully appointed with no hereditary peers

6 The following three reforms are in the process of being implemented:

- reducing its size by 10%
- giving constituents the power of recall
- giving MPs more power over parliamentary business

7 Any three of the following ways:

- vetoing legislation
- amending legislation against the government's wishes
- calling government to account and criticising its action
- select committees can reveal undesirable aspects of government
- questioning the prime minister and other ministers

Chapter 7

Now test yourself

1

Function	Cabinet	Prime minister	Minister
Conducting foreign policy		✓	
Determining policy presentation	✓		
Appointing cabinet ministers		✓	
Managing government departments			✓
Settling disputes between ministers	✓		
Guiding legislation through Parliament			✓
Commander-in-chief		✓	
Debating major crises	✓		

2

Power	Permanent	Variable
Commander-in-chief	✓	
Policy making		✓
Patronage	✓	
Conducting foreign policy	✓	
Controlling the cabinet		✓

3

Feature	Prime minister	President	Both
Responsible directly to the people		✓	
Elected separately from the government		✓	
Can be removed from office by his or her party	✓		
Has powers of patronage			✓
Conducts foreign policy			✓
Accountable to the legislature	✓		
Is *primus inter pares*	✓		
Is head of state		✓	
Is commander-in-chief			✓

Check your understanding

1 Any three of the following powers:
- making official government policy
- appointing and dismissing ministers and reshuffling the cabinet
- commanding the armed forces
- negotiating with foreign powers, including concluding treaties with them
- acting as a spokesman for the whole government
- leading the nation in crises and emergencies

2 Any three of the following limitations:
- may be overruled by the cabinet
- may be outvoted in Parliament
- may be removed from office by his or her party
- devolution limits his or her power over national regions
- power is limited by his or her popular and media reputation
- events outside the PM's control may limit his or her power

3 Any three of the following roles:
- to ratify policy proposals produced elsewhere
- to settle disputes between ministers
- occasionally to develop government policy
- to make decisions in a crisis or emergency
- to determine the presentation of government policy
- to give government policy collective legitimacy

4 Collective responsibility means that all ministers must defend government policy and are collectively responsible for it. Ministers who break the convention must resign or expect to be dismissed.

Individual ministerial responsibility requires ministers to be responsible for all the decisions and actions of their department. In extreme circumstances they may be required to resign over serious errors or over their own personal conduct.

5 Any three of the following reasons for resignation:
- a serious error made within their department
- problems with their personal conduct
- because they disagree with official government policy
- because they have serious differences with the prime minister
- when they feel their useful career is over

6 A head of government is normally elected alongside the other leading members of his or her party whereas a head of state is separately elected or is a hereditary monarch. Heads of government represent a temporary majority, whereas a head of state represents the whole nation.

A head of state is accountable directly to the people whereas a head of government usually accounts to a representative assembly. Heads of state can represent the nation abroad, while heads of government have a more limited role in this respect.

7 Any appropriate ministerial resignations can be used, but the following are prominent examples:
- Estelle Morris, Education Secretary, resigned in 2002 over schools' failure to meet their targets.
- Robin Cook resigned as Home Secretary in 2003 in opposition to the Iraq war.
- Clare Short, Development Secretary, resigned in 2003 over a similar issue.
- James Purnell, Pensions Secretary, resigned in 2009, having lost faith in Gordon Brown as prime minister.
- Jacqui Smith, Home Secretary, resigned in 2009 over problems with her MP's expenses claims.

8 The three main prerogative powers are:
- commanding the armed forces
- negotiating with foreign powers
- appointing and dismissing ministers

Chapter 8

Now test yourself

1

Feature	Independence	Neutrality
There should be a balance of men and women in the senior judiciary.		✓
The Supreme Court has been separated from Parliament.	✓	
Many senior judges were educated privately.		✓

Feature	Independence	Neutrality
Judges may not be active members of a political party.		✓
Judges have security of tenure.	✓	
The Judicial Appointments Commission appoints senior judges.	✓	✓

2

Fact	True	False
The Lord Chancellor is head of the judiciary.		✓
EU law is not binding on the UK Parliament.		✓
The European Court of Justice enforces the European Convention on Human Rights.		✓
Parliament can set minimum prison sentences for specific crimes.	✓	
The Supreme Court can declare a UK law invalid if it conflicts with the ECHR.		✓

3 (a) Privacy/freedom of expression

(b) Freedom of movement/expression

(c) Freedom of association

(d) Freedom of movement

Check your understanding

1 Any three of the following prominent examples:
- freedom of expression and the press
- freedom of thought and belief
- freedom of movement
- freedom of association
- freedom from detention without trial

2 Any two of the following reasons:
- A minister or public institution may have exceeded its legal powers.
- An action by a minister or public body may have offended the European Convention on Human Rights.
- Correct procedures for making decisions may not have been followed by a public institution.
- A public body may have acted against the principles of 'natural justice'.
- A citizen may claim to be the victim of unequal treatment by a public body.

3 The ECJ is the highest court in the European Union whereas the ECHR is the appeal court of the Council of Europe, guardian of the European Convention on Human Rights. The ECJ deals with disputes over EU law and disputes between EU member states, while the ECHR has no standing in the European Union.

4 The following are important human rights cases:
- super-injunctions secured by British celebrities
- the Belmarsh case concerning detention of terrorist suspects without trial
- the Afghan hijackers' case concerning rights of asylum

5 Any three of these:
- They interpret the meaning of laws.
- They declare and interpret common law.
- They make precedents which are binding on other courts.
- They make case law, demonstrating how laws should be applied in particular cases.

6 Any three of the following ways:
- Judges cannot be dismissed as a result of their decisions.
- Their salaries are guaranteed.
- Politicians have virtually no influence over senior appointments to the judiciary.
- The Supreme Court is politically independent.
- Ministers and MPs may not comment on ongoing legal cases.

7 The three main aspects of judicial neutrality are:
- Judges must not be politically active.
- Judges must be legally qualified.
- Judges must show no political or social bias in their decisions.